FUEL

The Energy You Need to Succeed

Wes Beavis

POWERBORN

This book contains the personal opinions and ideas of the author. It is not intended to be a substitute for gaining specific professional advice from legal, tax, investment, accounting, insurance, or financial advisors. It is the reader's responsibility to consult professional advice or services with regard to any strategies outlined in this book and to determine their relevance to the reader's geographical location and personal situation The contents of this book in no way dilute the absolute responsibility of the reader to perform due diligence with regard to any transactions nor do they absolve the reader from, or assign to the author or publisher, responsibility for the consequences of any actions taken.

FUEL : The Energy You Need to Succeed
by Wes Beavis

Copyright © 2009 W. J. Beavis

MANUFACTURED IN THE UNITED STATES OF AMERICA BY
Delta Printing Solutions
Valencia, California

10   9   8   7   6   5   4

COPYRIGHT & PUBLISHING ADMINISTRATION
POWERBORN - Irvine, California USA 92602
www.WesBeavis.com

For information about special discounts for quantity orders
contact POWERBORN by going to:
www.WesBeavis.com

Library of Congress Cataloging-in-Publication Data

Beavis, Wesley James.
FUEL : The Energy You Need to Succeed / Wes Beavis
     p.   cm.
1. Success in business– United States.   2. Quality of life– United States.
3. Work & Family– United States.   4. Self-actualization /
Maturation (Psychology)
I. Title   158.1 BEA —dc20   2009

ISBN-13: 978-1-888741-12-4
ISBN-10: 1-888741-12-0

Dedicated to the life of

Charlie 'Tremendous' Jones

A man whose fuel continues to burn brightly in my life.

Also by the Author

Become the Person You Dream of Being
Dating the Dream
Escape to Prosperity
Give Your Life a Success Makeover
Go and Be Successful

Contents

Introduction

You don't need the right conditions to succeed. You just need the right fuel. It does not matter if the times are good or bad. All that matters is whether you have the energy needed to achieve your dreams.

As I write, it seems every economic indicator is negative and plummeting. From what they say, we have sailed right into the perfect economic storm—a financial squall the size of which we haven't seen since the 1930's. Even more than a time for battling the elements, for some it will become the perfect excuse. Many will use these difficult times as justification for dry-docking themselves, doing nothing while waiting for the conditions to improve.

In the years to come, the economic times will have improved. Perhaps by the time you are reading this book, the hard times will have subsided. People will no longer use the rationale that conditions are not conducive for advancement. By then they will likely say that the playing field is too crowded and the competition too stiff. This book will be just as relevant. Because the reality is that success is the result of what is inside a person rather than what is happening in the world at the time. Successful people figure that out. Best of times, worst of times, and all of the times in between, it's not the conditions outside of you but the conditions inside of you that will lead you to succeed.

Gravity consistently works to inhibit any rocket from getting off the ground. The only question is whether the rocket has enough fuel to propel it beyond the power of gravity's containment. The fuel inside the rocket is more important than the gravitational force outside of it.

In rocket terms, many people are waiting for an absence of gravity before they launch. Or they blame gravity for their lack of upward movement: "Man, if it wasn't for that gravity, I would be in outer space by now!" No wonder they never get off the ground. Opposing forces are here to stay. They never let up. They reside equally potent and persuasive in both good times and hard times. The only question is, "Do you have sufficient fuel to propel yourself through opposing forces?"

People don't become successful because they sneak through a loophole or find an easy route. Rather they become successful because they learn how to fill up with enough fuel to propel them right through whatever forces are working to keep them contained. Their success and energy levels come by way of their fuel, not the absence of opposition.

So what is this fuel? Where do you get it? In the pages that follow, I will help you to locate and fill up with all the fuel that you need to succeed. As with every book I have written, this book is the result of what I have discovered to produce satisfying and lasting results. *FUEL: The Energy You Need to Succeed* will empower you, whatever the shape of your current conditions.

Add Fuel!

I was still enjoying the novelty of driving my newly acquired vehicle when something happened that I wasn't expecting. Driving down the road, a subtle alarm sounded that drew my attention to the onboard computer screen.

There, flashing before me, were the words 'Add Fuel.'
I glanced over at the fuel gauge and sure enough my fuel
tank was in need of replenishment.

I could have used that reminder a few years ago. At
that time, I was driving a rental car and making my way
back to the airport in Des Moines, Iowa. I had prepaid the
rental car company for a full tank of gas, so the aim was to
return the vehicle empty. Why give the rental company
half a tank of fuel for which I had already paid? I thought
it would be fun to return the rental car with only fumes in
the tank. If only I had considered the thought of how
pathetic it would be to run out of gas two miles short of
the airport with no fuel station in sight. That's exactly what
happened. Can you picture Wes Beavis pushing a rental
car down the road with a quickly fading hope of making
his flight?

Perhaps the rental car should have had a series of
audible messages: "Driver, you may want to consider refueling when it is convenient." Further down the road, the
message could be elevated to: "Driver, I would advise you
to make refueling a priority." If unheeded, the warning
could be raised to the rental car DEFCON 3 level: "Hey
buddy, get your head out of the clouds and get some gas
or you'll soon be walking!" Fortunately I have not run out
of fuel since that day in Des Moines, but there is still
something comforting about my new car reminding me
to 'add fuel.'

I am also reminded not to forget to add fuel to my
spirit. For every day the mental fuel that keeps us moving
forward is being constantly depleted as we push through
the challenging forces standing between us and our goal.
Too many people wait until they are chugging and
sputtering before admitting that they are running danger-

ously low on fuel. If your goal is a sizeable one, you're not going to make it on your current tank of fuel. Everyone, including me, learns that the hard way when they are broken down on the side of life's journey groaning, "This can't be happening!"

Waiting until you are out of gas before filling your tank is a very inefficient way of getting anywhere. The key to staying energized and succeeding is in your fuel management—knowing where to get fuel and filling up with as much as you can at every opportunity.

The study of success dynamics can be made complicated and overwhelming. Having spent decades living the subject, I have sought to distill from the vastness of information the critical factors. I have also worked to put these factors into a form that can be memorized. I have presented the vital factors as seven words beginning with the letter R (my apologies to those reading this in a language other than English). It is not an attempt to be cute or clever but an effort to give you something that easily chisels into the granite of your mind. I want you to have an unfading reference to your fuel sources. Here are the seven R's. Consider them seven fuel stations that will keep you mentally topped up.

1. Recommitment
2. Reading
3. Resources
4. Realizations
5. Relationships
6. Results
7. Rest

1

Recommitment
to the Essentials

1. Recommitment
to the Essentials

———∽∾∽———

What are the essentials?

     A. Attitude

     B. Belief

     C. Confidence

     D. Drive

     E. Enthusiasm

     F. Focus

You may read the list and think that there's nothing new here. Nothing you don't already know. You may be thinking, 'I have tried them all.' The key is not in knowing them. The key is not in trying them. The key is not agreeing with their importance. The key to unlocking the fuel contained within each of these essentials is the daily recommitting to them.

Get up every morning and run through the list in your mind. Imagine each one of these essentials has a gauge on your mental instrument panel. Just as an aircraft pilot checks his instrument panel before taking off, so we should 'tap the glass' on each gauge. How is my attitude? What is my level of belief in myself and what I represent? How's my confidence? Do I have drive? Can people see my enthusiasm? Am I focusing effectively? Yesterday's fuel is probably not enough to get you through today. Even though you topped up with a positive attitude yesterday, your tank may have run dry in the time since then. You may have started the week with confidence, but now it is Wednesday and you have probably burned a lot of fuel overcoming some rejections since the weekend.

Successful people recommit to these six essentials every day. The essentials are always crucial. They're not mental exercises you employ until you breakthrough to some nirvana level where they are no longer necessary. Many a person who has attained great heights of success has nose-dived because they didn't think they needed to pay attention to the essentials anymore. Become proficient at monitoring your fuel tank.

Would a pilot undertake a flight without sufficient fuel to get there? Would an astronaut climb into a rocket saying, "Hmm, a quarter of a tank? Yeah, that should be enough!" Seeing a prospect, contacting a client, or making sales calls with your 'low fuel' light flashing is risking a crash landing. The key to avoiding crash landings is to ensure you have enough fuel so that you can push right through the inevitable turbulence between you and your goal.

So let's do a refresher course on the six essentials and rediscover why they are a critical form of energy for every person in pursuit of their goals.

A. Attitude

The greatest discovery of any generation is that a
human being can alter his life by altering his attitude.
William James

—◦◦◦—

Whether you are heading for success or heading
for failure, your attitude will help you get there. Your
attitude can either fill your fuel tank or shoot holes in it.
The better your attitude, the more energy you will have.
A positive attitude can change your circumstances to be
more favorable. And if it can't change your circumstances,
a positive attitude will help you to transcend them.

It was a week before Christmas. My son Zack was
making a big effort to connect his video camera to his
computer. He called me while I was driving home and
asked if I could take him to the store to buy a special con-
nector. My pace quickened. I wanted to get home quickly
to help my son get his computer issue resolved. As I pulled
into our gated community, I was two turns away from
home when I saw a motorcycle police officer monitoring
people's response to a stop sign. My immediate thought
was, "What's he doing in a gated community? Shouldn't

he be outside in the real world catching genuine criminals?" It didn't matter. Although I had tapped the brakes and slowed down considerably, the officer had clearly seen me ooze through the stop sign without coming to a full and complete stop. I was guilty. I didn't even wait for him to get on his motorcycle and chase me around our gated community. I immediately pulled over. He simply walked across the road and sternly asked for my driver's license and registration papers.

I did a quick mental calculation and figured it had been fourteen years since my last moving violation. It was close to Christmas and I wondered if I could win the police officer over with a great attitude. I used my best motivational lines in the hope that I could escape with a warning. In the heat of the moment, the material I was coming up with was brilliant. I was getting motivated just listening to myself! But it did not work. The officer was unmoved, unmotivated, and just plain unwilling to do anything other than give me a ticket and an invitation to an eight hour session at traffic school.

As I pulled away I wondered whether my effort to enamor the police office with a good attitude was a waste of time. It certainly did not derive me a favorable response from him. Driving away, I was so tempted to slide into negativity. I was in danger of inflicting more damage to myself than the damage of the actual ticket. The words of Hugh Downs helped me to gain perspective: "A happy person is not a person in a certain set of circumstances, but rather a person with a certain set of attitudes." So I resolved to arrest my negative attitude which was quickly draining me of life. I reminded myself that though the police officer was wearing a gun, his power was limited to writing me a ticket, not writing me a destiny.

Although a positive and constructive attitude can win favorable responses, it is much more than that. When circumstances do not yield to match your positive disposition, your attitude empowers you to transcend the negativity of your circumstances. My good attitude did not stop the police officer from issuing me a ticket. But it did stop me from spreading the punishment to every other area of my life as I left the scene. Attitudes determine whether difficult occasions produce a profit or a loss. The choice is always ours.

The Anatomy of Attitude

What exactly is an attitude? Simply, your disposition in the way you process life and respond to issues. Your attitude can be anything from Hawaiian sunshine to a Siberian ice storm. For most people, attitude is governed by outside forces or emotions rather than a calculated decision. Making a conscious decision to be positive, regardless of the circumstances, is how to get energizing fuel flowing into your tank.

Your attitude can be influenced by the attitudes of others but ultimately no one can force you to have a particular attitude. Not only does Viktor Frankl, the Austrian neurologist and psychiatrist, sum it up best, but as a death camp Holocaust survivor, he is qualified to say it: "Everything can be taken from a man but one thing; the last of the human freedoms—to choose one's attitude in any given set of circumstances, to choose one's own way."

You have the right to choose your attitude every time in response to every issue. Admittedly, it can require a mental effort. You may have grown up in a family that modeled a certain way of responding to issues. By the process of osmosis, you have learned to respond the same way. But what is acceptable within the confines of your family may work against you in the wider world. You have to restyle your attitudes.

You may have a personality temperament that leans you towards certain emotional responses. You have to arrest your emotions and stop them from dictating your attitudes. Your basic temperament may be the poorest guide to a good attitude. Don't trust your temperament to set your attitude in the right direction.

Sometimes our responses are governed by what has worked in the past. Yet, past results may not guarantee future performance! How you responded when you were a teenager may be detrimental as an adult. Attitudes are too important to be governed by ingrained and function-ally automated mental patterns. You have to consciously form the right attitude every day and oftentimes reset your attitude during the day.

The Formation of an Attitude

The formation of a good attitude requires the awareness of your mental construction. If you owned land upon which you wanted to construct a building, most likely you would have to lodge plans with the city or local council to get a permit to construct the building. Primarily city officials want your building to be safe for the public and not detrimental to the overall formation of the com-munity. When you were born, your mind was like vacant land upon which you constructed a mental building. Our parents and teachers assisted us to build good minds, 'safe for the public and not detrimental to the community.'

Though we are taught and advised to have good minds, we do not have to apply for a permit to think the way we do. So it is up to us to be aware of our mental construction. Sometimes our mental construction is inadequate or even dangerous to our future. It's up to each individual to demolish and rebuild where necessary to become mentally more efficient. Many people end up with an uninspiring life not because of the lack of opportunity but because their mental construction is shabby.

Become aware of your response habits. Once you are aware of your responses, you can evaluate them and change them as necessary. The condition of your mental construction is the result of your efforts or lack of them. Your mind is a complex mental skyscraper but, with constant refurbishment and good management, it can project the right attitude into every situation.

The community I live in has covenants, conditions and restrictions (CC&R's) formulated to keep a certain quality standard in the community. For example, if my home needs painting I will receive a letter from the association asking me to repaint. If I fail to do so, they will hire a painting contractor to do it and send me the bill! They are not taking away my civic freedoms; they are ensuring that my community is well kept and protected from dilapidation that would lower the value of all of our homes. It's a valuable agreement beneficial to everyone. We should do the same with our minds. Establish covenants, conditions and restrictions for our mind that would not allow negative attitudes.

As I travel across various cities teaching the principles of life improvement, sometimes I throw in a song to reinforce an important point. The last thing I do before stepping onto the stage is to check that my guitar is in tune. Often the tension on the strings can shift with the rigors of travel or the temperature changes in locations. If my guitar is out of tune, it adversely affects my perform-ance. Our attitudes are like the strings of a guitar on the stage of life. Our performance will be much better if we stop and adjust our attitudes to be in tune. It's better to make the adjustments before we perform, but there will be times we need to make adjustments mid-performance.

Successful people constantly check their mental tuning. They process their issues through the filter of a good attitude. They know it is essential to keep adjusting their attitudes. Changing conditions can so easily negatively tweak one's thinking. The successful person has learned that a good attitude is powerful fuel for overcoming the inevitable obstacles. A good attitude costs nothing more to produce than a bad one and is far more productive in helping you achieve your goals. Take charge of your attitudes and in turn they will keep you charged.

—ⲟⲛⲟ—

Now to the How To: Attitude

1. Eliminate the notion that good attitudes come naturally. They are the product of effort for everyone. Acknowledge that good mental responses require a daily commitment to achieving them and keeping them.

2. Start each day with the words, "How I respond to the issues of today is up to me. May I be found to be with a good attitude at every turn." Write this on a card and carry it with you.

3. If you have an attitude lapse, don't punish yourself and relegate yourself to the scrap heap of failure. Forgive yourself and ask the forgiveness of others. Acknowledge that you are a work in progress and that all improvement takes practice and persistence.

4. If you have hot buttons which 'set you off', work out a mental strategy ahead of time for how to maintain calmness when one of those buttons is pushed. Master your hot buttons one at a time. Don't try and conquer them all at once.

5. At the end of the day review your attitude performance. Evaluate your attitudes and finish the day with the words: "I will use today to make tomorrow better."

6. Negative feelings towards other people can become our greatest source of stress. Replace negative feelings about certain people with positive thoughts about them. This will stop the leakage of your emotional energy and help you to regain joy about life.

7. Find a friend who also wants to improve in this area. Make a commitment to keep each other accountable to a higher standard in attitude.

Quick Fuel: Attitude

Your living is determined not so much by what life brings to you as by the attitude you bring to life; not so much by what happens to you as by the way your mind looks at what happens. *Kahlil Gibran*

If you don't like something change it; if you can't change it, change the way you think about it. *Mary Engelbreit*

Very often a change of self is needed more than a change of scene. *Arthur Christopher Benson*

The most successful people are those who are good at plan B. *James Yorke*

Be pleasant until ten o'clock in the morning and the rest of the day will take care of itself. *Elbert Hubbard*

Man is made or unmade by himself. In the armory of thought he forges the weapons by which he destroys himself. *James Allen*

A positive attitude causes a chain reaction of positive thoughts, events and outcomes. It is a catalyst and it sparks extraordinary results. *Wade Boggs*

Good fortune shies away from gloom. Keep your spirits up. Good things will come to you and you will come to good things. *Glorie Abelhas*

Every day may not be good, but there's something good in every day. *Unknown*

We cannot change our past. We cannot change the fact that people act in a certain way. We cannot change the inevitable. The only thing we can do is play on the one string we have, and that is our attitude. *Charles R. Swindoll*

Things turn out best for the people who make the best out of the way things turn out. *Art Linkletter*

Success Workshop: Attitude

1. Does having a positive attitude come easily for you or do you have to work at it? Indicate it on the scale.

Takes effort   Comes easily

2. What are the 'low fuel' indicators that tell you that you're in need of an attitude top-up?

_____

_____

3. What things are the most effective in filling up your attitude tank?

_____

_____

4. What things are most likely to shoot holes in your attitude tank?

_____

5. List three people who you admire for their responses to life's issues.

_____

6. Name a difficult circumstance and then come up with a positive way to respond.

_____

_____

_____

B. Belief

Nothing splendid has ever been achieved except by
those who dared believe that something inside of
them was superior to circumstances.
Bruce Barton

———∽∽∽———

Belief and doubt are like two tour guides, each
vying for your attention on the road of life. Where you
end up depends on who you listened to the most. People
who excel in life are not the ones who eliminate doubt
but the ones who conquer the natural tendency of being
double minded. Everyone knows they have potential for
greatness. It's just that many keep sabotaging their belief
with a mental intravenous drip that administers constant
doses of doubt.

Imagine you are a ship with two captains. One
captain takes the daylight hours and the other the night
hours. How far would you get if each captain begins his
day by promptly reversing the course of the other? It's not
the absence of belief that stops an individual's advance
but the presence of double-mindedness. Being led by
belief and doubt ultimately leads you to frustration and
wrong conclusions about your ability.

Success requires you to both believe in yourself and overcome double-mindedness. As James Allen wrote, "Doubts and fears should be rigorously excluded. They are disintegrating elements which break up the straight line of effort, rendering it crooked, ineffectual, useless. Thoughts of doubt and fear never accomplish anything, and never can."

The Anatomy of Belief

What exactly is belief? It's your level of trust that you put in something or someone. Belief in yourself is simply the level of trust you have in your potential. We start our lives with an infinite belief in ourselves. Cry and someone feeds you. If you feel uncomfortable, cry again and people will put you in some fresh pants. You think, 'Wow, this is great life. Squawk and I get attention!'

Then as we grow, reality starts to erode some of our beliefs. We have to start changing our own pants. And then we even have to replace them with our own money! We stop believing that we are going to be super heroes, princesses, and movie stars. In fact, having been subdued by enough reality, we stop believing we are capable of anything exceptional. We stop believing we are special and start putting ourselves 'on sale,' selling ourselves at a discounted rate to anyone who will pay us a secure wage. As someone once said, "If you put a small value upon yourself, rest assured that the world will not raise your price."

Your actions will inevitably follow your beliefs. So if you believe that you're average then you will act average, attract average, and everything about your life will become average. Your life will eventually reflect your beliefs and those beliefs will help you find reasons to justify your place in life. If you want to improve your life you must improve your belief in yourself. Your life will never go beyond what you believe you can make possible.

The Formation of Belief

Forget waiting for others to believe in you. It is not going to happen. Sometimes I hear a person saying of those who have encouraged them in their journey: "They believed in me before I believed in myself!" It's a nice sentiment but if you hang the hopes of your future on someone believing in you before you believe in yourself, you're going to die waiting. Even if you are supremely lucky to have someone give you an encouraging 'jump start,' they will quickly move on if you fail to hold the charge and don't start moving under your own energy.

Here's the reality: Ultimately people will not believe in you beyond your belief in yourself. Most times, to even gain the belief of others you must first believe in yourself. Marianne Williamson said it best: "Maturity includes the recognition that no one is going to see anything in us that we do not see in ourselves. Stop waiting for a producer. Produce yourself."

Belief finds its basis in what you see. Do you see yourself being in a better position? Do you see someone doing great things and wish that were you? Do you see better conditions and ask yourself, "Why not me?" You 'see' because your potential is trying to get your attention. If you did not have the potential for these things, you wouldn't see them or even care enough to take notice. The fact that you see a better life is proof that you have the latent ability to bring what you see into reality. Start believing that you have the ability to bring what you see into reality. If you see it, believe it and rip out that mental intravenous drip that administers constant doses of doubt. Belief is the fuel that propels potential into reality.

It is a fact of human nature that we tend to credit others with having more ability than they actually do and credit ourselves with having less ability than we actually do. Except for the occasional narcissist, we all tend to depreciate ourselves way below our true value. The truth is that we have a long way to go before being in danger of overestimating what we can achieve. Most people operate way below what they are capable. They continue to 'see' opportunity but their doubts have so drained their tank of belief that they don't have the fuel to go after what they see. Buckminster Fuller sums it up: "I am convinced all of humanity is born with more gifts than we know. Most are born geniuses and just get de-geniused rapidly."

It doesn't cost you anything to stop doubting and start believing. In fact, the opportunity cost of being continually guided by your doubts can be immense. Ask any elderly person and they will likely tell you that the regret of their non-adventures far outweighs the pain brought on by any misadventure. Take a shot on believing that you have more inside of you than what you are giving yourself credit. Start believing that you are capable of more and validate that belief by acting on it. As David Schwartz said, "Successful people are just ordinary folks who have developed belief in themselves and what they do."

Your mind is one big computer processor. It works with the information that is fed into it. Whatever you believe or doubt, your mind will automatically set about finding reasons to support your conclusions. Bombard your mind with thoughts of self-belief. Trick your mind. Without doubts, your onboard computer will have no alternative but to work with your beliefs. Get rid of all your doubt-default settings. You are not naturally prone to failure. You have simply let too much doubt and wrong assumptions fill up your mental hard drive. No one has ever doubted themselves into a better future.

When you set your mind to believing in yourself rather than doubting yourself, your actions will start lining up with that belief. Your creative capacity will start coming up with breakthrough ideas. Other people will start to believe about you what you believe about yourself. Your income will start reflecting your beliefs. If you see yourself creating more income, it is because your potential to earn more is trying to get your attention. Don't let your self-doubts continue to hijack your guidance system. Re-boot with belief. Believe that the future will be better. Believe that you have what it takes to make the future brighter. What do you see? What can you imagine? Take heed of what you see for it is evidence of your potential. Believing in yourself is the fuel that your potential needs to transport you to what you see.

—◦◦◦—

Now to the How To: Belief

1. When you see something that appeals to you, don't ignore it. Recognize that your potential tries to get your attention through your eyes.

2. Be aware that belief suffers at the hands of double-mindedness just as much as doubt. Don't be a ship with two captains. Choose your captain and let him captain.

3. Form an image of who you want to be in three years time and start acting like that person now.

4. Use your mouth to establish your beliefs. Make a list of things you will start to believe about yourself. Every day, say out loud what you believe about yourself.

Quick Fuel: Belief

Your most important sale in life is to sell yourself to yourself. *Maxwell Maltz*

The outer conditions of a person's life will always be found to reflect their inner beliefs. *James Allen*

Once you become self-conscious, there is no end to it; once you start to doubt, there is no room for anything else. *Mignon McLaughlin*

If you believe you can, you probably can. If you believe you won't, you most assuredly won't. Belief is the ignition switch that gets you off the launching pad. *Denis Waitley*

Men often become what they believe themselves to be. If I believe I cannot do something, it makes me incapable of doing it. But when I believe I can, then I acquire the ability to do it even if I didn't have it in the beginning. *Mahatma Gandhi*

What lies behind us and what lies before us are tiny matters compared to what lies within us. *Ralph Waldo Emerson*

Perseverance isn't just the willingness to work hard. It's that plus the willingness to be stubborn about your own belief in yourself. *Merlin Olsen*

Within you right now is the power to do things you never dreamed possible. This power becomes available to you just as you can change your beliefs. *Maxwell Maltz*

To move ahead you need to believe in yourself. . . have conviction in your beliefs and the confidence to execute those beliefs. *Adlin Sinclair*

Men harm others by their deeds, themselves by their thoughts. *Augustus William Hare and Julius Charles Hare*

Laugh at yourself, but don't ever aim your doubt at yourself. Be bold. When you embark for strange places, don't leave any of yourself safely on shore. Have the nerve to go into unexplored territory. *Alan Alda*

Success Workshop: Belief

1. On the following scale, indicate your self-belief:

Low   High

2. Why does doubt come so easily?

_____

_____

3. What are the doubts that grip you the most?

_____

_____

4. Where did those doubts come from?

_____

5. I determine to believe the following about myself:

_____

6. I am going to take the following actions to validate believing in myself:

_____

_____

7. As of this date _____, I commit to believing that I have more ability within me than I have explored or developed. Even when times are tough, I will believe that I am even tougher. I renounce the limiting power that my doubts have had over me.

C. Confidence

The self-confidence of a person multiplies
their powers a hundredfold.
Robert Collier

———⟞◦⟊◦⟝———

I have never forgotten something that happened
to me when I was young. My father's new job required our
family to relocate to a new town thousands of miles away.
Upon enrolling in school, word spread quickly that my
older brother could run as fast as a jackrabbit. I was in
class when the track coach asked my teacher if he could
see me outside for a few minutes. He talked excitedly
about discovering my brother's running ability and he
seemed exceptionally interested in me. He told me to
follow him, whereby he led me onto a field where he had
assembled the fastest runners in the school. Hoping that
I could deliver the same swiftness as my older brother, the
coach had organized a running race to determine whether
the school was fortunate enough to have lightning strike
twice in the same family.

The pressure was on. I knew my running pace was
nowhere near as fast as my brother's. I secretly hoped that

we had moved to a town of slow pokes or that something in the mid-west air would give me the legs of a gazelle. The coach yelled, "Ready. Set. Go!" The race was on. My effort was valiant but not enough to stop everyone crossing the finish line before me. The race was over and with it the coach's interest in me. He told us to go back to our respective classes. He offered praise to the race winners but never spoke to me again. I went back to class having lost a whole lot more than the race. Somewhere out on that field, gasping for breath, lay my confidence. I returned to the classroom without it.

Surely every person reading this book could match my experience with their own version. It seems confidence is so hard to build and yet so easy to lose. How you feel about yourself can quickly turn into a pile of rubble after one social earthquake. I doubt that track coach would have remembered the incident beyond that day but thirty-six years later, I remember it as if it happened yesterday! Fortunately, over the last thirty-six years I have also learned what it takes to build confidence and protect it. For no one succeeds without it. A person's success is in direct proportion to their confidence.

The Anatomy of Confidence

Confidence is having certainty. It is where the debris of doubt, fear, and insecurity is swept off the table of your mind, leaving only certainty with which to reconcile a situation. Self-confidence is having faith in your ability to handle issues. Some people exude so much confidence you would think that they were born with it. The reality is far from that. Even though some people may exude all the confidence in the world, it's no proof that they actually have it. They may just be good actors like acclaimed comedian Arsenio Hall who confessed, "I don't possess a lot of self-confidence. I'm an actor so I simply act confident every time I hit the stage. I am consumed with the fear of failing. Reaching deep down and finding confidence has made all my dreams come true." Confidence is not something that you are born with. You build it. And having built it, protect it, and don't neglect it.

The Formation of Confidence

There's no need to convince you of the benefits of confidence. We all know that we are a hundred times better with it than without it. As Marcus Garvey said, "If you have no confidence in self, you are twice defeated in the race of life. With confidence, you have won even before you have started." There are several ways to build and protect your confidence. Employ each one of them.

1. Affirm yourself

The primary key to confidence is liking yourself. All other confidence building efforts will eventually crumble under the weight of your self-loathing. We all have reasons to be down on ourselves. When we focus on them, we are effectively sabotaging our confidence. Don't wait to like yourself before you start liking yourself. That day will never come. Decide to like yourself, for better or for worse, today! Build up your confidence by saying (fill in your name), "_____, I like you!" Say it several times often throughout the day and especially when you hit a rough patch. Try it, it works!

2. Affirm the day

As you affirm yourself, affirm the day. Get up each morning and say, "This is a great day to succeed!" You take command of the day. Don't let circumstances set your mood. You set the tone. Even on the worst day, you always have the last say by how you respond. Your power to influence the day is stronger than you think. Affirm the day as a great one. It will move towards that affirmation.

3. The development and recognition of ability

Refine your ability to the point where it makes a noteworthy impression and attracts the affirmations of others. If you spend ten thousand hours developing any skill valued in the marketplace, you will become an expert and likely be recognized as such. It is a slow way to build confidence but, if you stay the course, you will eventually shower in the praises of people. You will be fueled by their confidence in you.

4. Priming the pump with acting

Start acting confidently. Success is quite undiscerning. It gravitates towards confidence, even if a person is just 'acting' confident in the absence of real confidence. Success is more likely to come to the person who lacks the ability but conjured up the confidence to try than to the person who actually has the ability but lacks the confidence to try.

You cannot fake success but you can fake the confidence that attracts success to you. Donald Trump says it this way: "Even if you haven't encountered great success yet, there is no reason you can't bluff a little and act like you have. Confidence is a magnet in the best sense of the word. It will draw people to you and make your daily life and theirs. . . a lot more pleasant."

Confidence has a way of trouncing talent. The person with less talent and more confidence will go further than someone who has significant talent coupled with timidity. It's not fair but that's the way that it is. Confidence has a self-fulfilling prophecy element to it. Opportunity is enamored by confidence.

Opportunity opens doors to the confident. So act confident, even when you're not. But don't forget to prepare your skills as well. Confidence can get the door opened but your skills and talent can get you invited in. Be guided by the words of George Herbert: "Skill and confidence is an unconquered army."

5. Surviving failure

Failure can impact your confidence but *surviving* a failure gives you more self-confidence. People fear failure because they think it will be the death of them. But failure can have the opposite effect. When you get to the other side of a failure and realize that you still have a pulse, you recognize that you must have been stronger than you previously estimated. Your confidence in your survivorship increases. If you survive a gargantuan failure, your respect for your survival capacity increases even more.

Too many people sabotage their confidence by incessantly beating themselves up for past mistakes. Direct that energy towards learning from them and feel your confidence rise. You are much stronger than you think. Eleanor Roosevelt summed it up: "You gain strength, courage, and confidence by every experience by which you really stop to look fear in the face. You are able to say to yourself, I lived through this horror. I can take the next thing that comes along."

With the right response, failures can be the making of your confidence. Counterbalance your failure with some success too. If all you know is failure, your confidence will choke on the bones of constant disappointment. Failure, like debt, is not necessarily bad unless that is all your balance sheet reflects. Don't be afraid of failure but also strive to keep it to a manageable minimum.

6. Being the last one standing

Admittedly, the race usually goes to the swift and the strong but not always. Sometimes you will receive the prize just by outlasting everyone else. Just ask Steven Bradbury. He was a speed skater in the men's short track 1000 meters final at the 2002 Winter Olympic Games in Salt Lake City. Hopelessly skating in last place, he took the final turn just in time to see the leader of the race crash to the ice, taking the second, third and fourth place skaters with him. Steven Bradbury, who was skating in fifth place, was so far behind the pack that he had time to avoid the pile up. He skated across the finish line, solo, winning the gold medal.

Sometimes all you need to do is just outlast your competition. It is confidence building to know that you're still standing when so many others have fallen over. As William Feather once said, "Success seems to be largely a matter of hanging on after others have let go."

7. Dress up!

If you look like a pack mule people will load you up with their junk. The clothing with which you present yourself influences how people value you. Dress up! It is one of the simplest ways to elevate your confidence and feel good about yourself. Sometimes a new outfit is all you need to give your confidence a winning boost.

8. Never sacrifice your confidence to a critic

No one has succeeded without being criticized along the way. If there are some voices critical of you, don't give them the keys to your confidence. Most times people criticize in a fruitless attempt to bolster their own self esteem. It never works and neither does it work to our advantage to listen to them. As Sally Field once confessed, "It took me a long time not to judge myself through someone else's eyes." Nothing siphons off your energy quite like giving a critic access to your confidence.

9. Have a clear vision and definite plans

I was once flying over a mountain range in a light aircraft. It was a two-seater Cessna with my friend in the pilot's seat. The ride was significantly bumpy as we battled the updrafts and thermals. My pilot friend was doing his best controlling the steering with one hand and holding a map with the other. After several moments of looking at the map and straining to get a visual of the landscape, he turned to me and asked, "Do you see a landing strip anywhere out there?" I was already questioning my wisdom in taking the flight, that comment did nothing to bolster my confidence.

Often we suffer a confidence crisis because we lack direction. In the absence of a definite plan to follow, we drift around hoping that we are on track. You cannot feel confident and vulnerable at the same time. The most debilitating periods in my life have been when I have bounced around not sure where I am going or where I should land. While being hopeful is important, as John Maxwell says, "Hope is not a strategy." When you add to your hope a clear goal, backed by strategic plans, you become confident and powerful.

If you are lost in the airspace of uncertainty, staying there will only further erode your already depleted confidence. Humble yourself and get some guidance from someone successful. Pay them for their time if need be. Put together a plan. Once you have a plan, commit to it, and don't allow your feelings to second guess it. Having a clear map of directions will give you extraordinary confidence in the journey.

10. Accomplish something

If you want to improve your confidence, improve something. Achieve something that makes a difference. Dale Carnegie implores us to get off our behinds with the following: "Inaction breeds doubt and fear. Action breeds confidence and courage. If you want to conquer fear, do not sit home and think about it. Go out and get busy." Quit blaming your lack of confidence on things that have happened to you. Too often we lament life 'happening' to us. Make yourself 'happen' to life for a change. The street goes both ways. Go and impose yourself upon life in an area that needs improvement.

Confidence comes from accomplishment. It does not need to be a media-mesmerizing achievement. Zig Ziglar says, "If you can't do great things, do small things in a great way." Every small accomplishment eventually adds up to a confident life.

11. Be financially solvent

Our confidence is so influenced by our financial solvency or our lack of it. A lack of money so easily leads to a lack of confidence. And a lack of confidence so easily leads to a lack of money. It's a vicious cycle. I'm not saying to put your confidence in money. But I am saying you can smooth out the ups and downs of life with more confidence when you're not broke. Save up! Have a sizeable and readily accessible amount of money in your bank account. It will do wonders for your confidence.

12. Healthy friendships – Healthy environment

Confidence is not only something that you build but it is something that you must protect. Some friends can build your confidence and some can subtly erode it. Be aware of the influence that relationships have upon you. Limit your contact with people who have a negative effect on your confidence. If you must have contact with them, put your armor on before you see them. They may not deposit anything into your confidence account but you can stop them from swiping anything from your current balance. Gravitate towards people who inspire you rather than expire you!

The same goes for environments. Be aware of the impact that a physical environment can have on your confidence. A negative workplace may cause you to doubt your abilities. Some social settings may have you second guessing your value. Do not stay any longer than is absolutely necessary in an environment that depletes you.

Plan to be in positive friendships and environments. Unless you plan for good conditions you will get the leftovers by default. Quality rarely comes spontaneously. Be proactive in protecting your confidence by planning for healthy friendships and healthy environments.

13. Stop craving approval

We all want to feel accepted. It is human nature. When you dig deep into your subconscious, you will discover that a crash in self-confidence is often connected to feeling like you have lost people's approval. So hungry we can be for the approval of others that we try to protect our 'approval rating' by not risking it. We attempt to protect our confidence by not doing anything that could make us feel foolish. The reality is that being governed by a need for approval erodes your confidence. As Charles Schwab said, "The man who trims himself to suit everybody will soon whittle himself away."

Developing confidence requires you to step out of your comfort zone, try new things, and stretch yourself. Forget what the masses may think of you. Let your future be decided by your potential not by trying to preserve face with others. Frankly, other people are too busy trying to preserve themselves in the eyes of their peers to spend time thinking about you. Remember the words of Olin Miller, "We probably wouldn't worry about what people think of us if we could know how seldom they do."

14. Choose Confidence

As with attitude and belief, confidence is ultimately a choice. It does not cost you extra to employ it. Use all of the above ways to build your confidence and remember that you must choose to be confident regardless of whether you feel confident or not. Make a daily commitment to being a confident person. Not having faith in yourself never pays. Success is attracted to confidence and it rarely looks behind the curtain to examine the actual basis for that confidence. So fill up with confidence and by doing so, gain the energy you need to succeed.

Now to the How To: Confidence

1. Evaluate the above list of confidence builders and determine which ones can help you the most. Rank them in order of relevance to you, print them on a card, and carry it with you. Review the list of confidence builders at intervals during the day and let them work to build your confidence.

2. Commit to the understanding that your confidence level is your responsibility and that it is within your control.

3. Formulate a Confidence Plan. Do something every day that will work to building your confidence.

4. Build up your confidence by saying (fill in your name), "_____, I like you!" Make a list of personal qualities that you have and read them every day.

5. Do something which you have been afraid of doing.

6. Call or write someone and remind them of a quality that they possess that you admire. Do something to build their confidence.

Quick Fuel: Confidence

A man cannot be comfortable without his own approval. *Mark Twain*

If I have lost confidence in myself, I have the universe against me. *Ralph Waldo Emerson*

They are the weakest, however strong, who have no faith in themselves or their own powers. *Christian Bovee*

Life is not easy for any of us. But what of that? We must have perseverance and above all confidence in ourselves. We must believe that we are gifted for something and that this thing must be attained. *Marie Curie*

Confidence is contagious and so is lack of confidence, and a customer will recognize both. *Vincent Lombardi*

Confidence is the most important single factor in this game, and no matter how great your natural talent, there is only one way to obtain and sustain it: work.
Jack Nicklaus

A good leader inspires people to have confidence in the leader; a great leader inspires people to have confidence in themselves. *John C. Maxwell*

Confidence comes not from always being right but from not fearing to be wrong. *Peter T. McIntyre*

Regardless of how you feel inside, always try to look like a winner. Even if you are behind, a sustained look of control and confidence can give you a mental edge that results in victory. *Diane Arbus*

If you hear a voice within you say 'you cannot paint', then by all means paint, and that voice will be silenced.
Vincent Van Gogh

Success Workshop: Confidence

1. On the following scale, indicate the level of your self-confidence:

Low   High

2. Can you recall the first time you experienced a crash in confidence? Did it cause you to be more cautious? Have you become overly cautious?

_____

_____

_____

_____

3. In striving for your goal, what factor do you find the hardest? How could greater confidence help you?

_____

_____

4. What do you worry about the most in approaching a complete stranger? What is the worst thing that could happen? Could you survive it?

_____

_____

_____

_____

_____

5. If you walked into a room of strangers, what could you do to get to know ten new people?

_____

_____

_____

_____

7. Name three people in your life that you admire for their confidence. What gives you the impression that they are confident people?

_____

_____

_____

8. What in the list of twelve confidence builders could you immediately incorporate?

_____

_____

_____

_____

9. Are there any confidence builders not listed in the twelve that have helped you?

_____

_____

_____

_____

D. Drive

Success is almost totally dependent upon drive
and persistence. The extra energy required to
make another effort or try another approach
is the secret of winning.
Denis Waitley

———————

You can go all the way to the top with ordinary
talent and extraordinary drive. Infirmities and handicaps
bow their knee to personal drive. The ability to muster
oneself into action is the supreme ability of all abilities. It
is that drive which can fuel your efforts out of mediocrity
into success.

Some years ago while I was living in Australia,
the nation's economy was overheating. To curtail the
possibility of runaway inflation, the government increased
interest rates as a mechanism to 'cool' the overheating
economy. Yet the interest rate hikes were not having the
desired cooling effect. This was unfortunate for homeowners as there was no such thing as a thirty-year fixed
interest rate on a home mortgage. At that time no lenders
offered such terms. So every time the government raised

interest rates, homeowners' monthly mortgage payments went up. In two years, the interest rate on our home mortgage went from 8.75 to 19.25 percent. The repayments went through the roof. Eventually the economy cooled, but it was not until it was too late that the government realized that it had not only cooled the economy but killed it. Suffice to say, money became scarce.

Around that same time, my wife had resigned from her teaching position to give birth to our first child. We went from 'double income, no kids' to 'one income and three mouths to feed.' It was also during this time when the directors of the organization where I was employed decided to make an across the board salary cut in response to its diminishing financial reserves. Right there in the executive boardroom, I made a decision. I went home to Ellie and announced that I was going to resign and start my own business. I figured that if I was going to crash and burn financially, it should happen running my own business and not being the employee of someone else's.

So within the space of a few months, we went from 'double income, no kids' to 'zero income, three hungry people, and a huge home mortgage to feed.' Talk about debt propulsion! With the nation's recession continuing to march on, I was nervous, uncertain, and financially unprepared. Yes, I could have accepted the pay cut and somehow made it work. But there was something within me that said, "Don't let the hard times dictate your destiny. Don't sit back, go on the attack. Just because the nation is in a recession doesn't mean you have to be!" So, driven by a dream for something better than recessionary conditions, I hit the road with nowhere to go but up.

After a good season on the road, I discovered an opportunity that dramatically reversed my fortunes. It was a break that never would have come my way had I stayed with my previous employment and accepted the pay cut. It was an opportunity that was waiting for me to get motivated enough to get out there and 'stumble' upon it. Something in the midst of my family's gloomiest financial season, produced the most bountiful economic season we had ever experienced. That something was drive. It would not allow me to sit back and let hard times dictate the quality of my life.

Recessions will always come and go. Every time the wheel of business goes around, it travels through a section where the excesses of jubilant times are brought into line with historical norms. The danger of recessions is that people duck for cover and wait it out. A friend of mine responds this way, "We may be in a recession but I am choosing not to participate in it." That's the spirit of drive. Whatever tough times you are in, put yourself in drive mode and get through them. Whatever good times are ahead, put yourself in drive and get to them. The road to the mountain top is called Personal Drive.

The Anatomy of Drive

Drive is the ability to be self-motivated. Drive is not something that you are born with; it is something that is born within you. Hard times can birth it in you. A dream can birth it in you. Being passionate about something can produce extraordinary drive. If you get sick and tired of being sick and tired, chances are drive is forming within you. Often people raised in poverty develop tremendous drive to escape poverty. Debt propulsion drove me, but I was also fueled by the dream of a better life for my family.

The bottom line is that drive is essential to success. What musters you into action? What causes you to stay up late and get up early? Discover what drives you and nurture it.

The Formation of Drive

There are basically two motivating factors in life: the promise of pleasure and the fear of pain. Drive finds its basis in either or both. People will go to great lengths to avoid pain and equal lengths in the pursuit of pleasure. If you want to excel in life, the key is to exploit the motivating forces of either. In my case, I was motivated by both the fear of struggling to provide for my family and the dream of providing a prosperous life for my family. My drive came from the fear of being a caged employee for the rest of my life and the dream of having my own thriving business. I was both passionate about escaping the doldrums and hungry for something better. I knew clearly what I didn't want and had a clear vision for what I did want.

People may lack drive because they don't have a purpose which ignites their passion. People may lack drive because they have just enough success not to live in fear of pain. People may lack drive because they have just enough comfort to take away the hunger for something superior. Current success can be the limiting factor for future success because it reduces a person's drive. So, as you succeed you need to identify new causes that keep the drive in you. Country singer Eddie Rabbit once said that the key to his success was to live with one pocket empty and one pocket full. In other words, enjoy your successes but don't eliminate your need to keep producing value.

As with attitude, belief, and confidence, drive is a choice. If you lack drive, it's because you allowed yourself to settle. You have not cultivated the mental conditions that produce drive. You have allowed your external conditions to mellow you. Your impact in the world will never exceed your drive to have an impact. If you lack drive, something is wrong. Set about fixing it. As Arnold H. Glasow once said, "Success isn't a result of spontaneous combustion. You must set yourself on fire."

The right dream will come with the drive to make it happen. What ignites a fire within you? If dire circumstances are what you need to get you motivated, sit around long enough and dire circumstances will knock on your door. A compelling dream, however, often needs to be tracked down. Go out and find a dream that releases the drive within you to stay up late and get up early. Don't wait for one to come to you.

———∕⊘⊘∕———

Now to the How To: Drive

1. Evaluate whether your present place in life is the result of 'going with the flow' or creating the life that you want.

2. Identify what you are really passionate about.

3. Get rid of old dusty dreams that haven't materialized. Find yourself a new ambitious but achievable dream— something that invigorates you to 'fight gravity' every day.

4. Find a picture of that dream, laminate it, and carry it in your wallet or purse (in front of your driver's license!).

5. Tell yourself that there is no such thing as a lack of energy just the lack of a dream that inspires you to have drive.

6. Develop a new reputation among those who know you that you are a person with drive.

Quick Fuel: Drive

Without action an idea will never get any bigger than the brain cell it occupied. *Arnold H. Glasow*

Conditions are never just right. People who delay action until all factors are favorable do nothing. *William Feather*

It is never too late to be who you might have been. *George Eliot*

Empty pockets never held anyone back. Only empty heads and empty hearts can do that. *Norman Vincent Peale*

Good business leaders create a vision, articulate the vision, passionately own the vision, and relentlessly drive it to completion. *Jack Welch*

When I was young, I observed that nine out of ten things I did were failures. So I did ten times more work. *George Bernard Shaw*

A man can be as great as he wants to be. If you believe in yourself and have the courage, the determination, the dedication, the competitive drive and if you are willing to sacrifice the little things in life and pay the price for the things that are worthwhile, it can be done. *Vince Lombardi*

Things may come to those who wait, but only the things left by those who hustle. *Abraham Lincoln*

Getting ahead in a difficult profession requires avid faith in yourself. That is why some people with mediocre talent, but with great inner drive, go so much further than people with vastly superior talent. *Sophia Loren*

My passions were all gathered together like fingers that made a fist. Drive is considered aggression today; I knew it then as purpose. *Bette Davis*

Success Workshop: Drive

1. On the following scale, indicate the level of your personal drive:

Low   High

2. Would people say that personal drive is one of your qualities? Why or why not?

_____

_____

_____

3. Does your dream of yesterday fire you up like it used to? Is it time to get a new dream?

_____

4. Name three people who have surprised you with what they have accomplished, not by talent but by sheer drive?

_____

_____

_____

5. Having drive is a choice. List three ways that you can demonstrate an elevated level of personal drive.

_____

_____

_____

E. Enthusiasm

A person who lacks enthusiasm will
never develop it in another.
David Schwartz

It is not an abundance of problems that limits us but rather a lack of enthusiasm. Whatever the problem, the answer begins with your enthusiasm. An energetic spirit is the starting point for every achievement. As with attitude, belief, confidence, and drive, enthusiasm is your choice. You can switch it on or leave it off. Enthusiasm will not switch on automatically. It will not stay on automatically. It is a choice to be made daily.

Too many people wait until things go their way before they generate enthusiasm. Without the benefit of favorable conditions they are simply unwilling to muster any excitement. Not so with the successful. They radiate enthusiasm first. They don't wait for the right conditions. At some point in their lives they decided to make enthusiasm their default personality setting. They know that the field of life is biased towards those who can rally personal enthusiasm—regardless of what mess they're facing.

The Anatomy of Enthusiasm

Enthusiasm means that someone's whole-hearted devotion to something is expressed with energy and excitement. Simply put, being enthusiastic means having a vibrant spirit. Enthusiasm need never be conditional upon the conditions. It is a fountain that springs up from within, propelled by the belief that life is better met and better enjoyed with enthusiasm. As a personality trait, enthusiasm is an investment with a good return. It is the outward working of inner beliefs. If you don't believe in your product, service, abilities, opportunities, or your future, displaying enthusiasm will be virtually impossible.

The Formation of Enthusiasm

If you want to be an enthusiastic person you have to commit to enthusiasm as a way of life not as a response to favorable conditions. Do not make your enthusiasm conditional upon things going your way. Get up in the morning and recommit to being an enthusiastic person. Eliminate the erroneous assumption that some people are naturally more fervent. Stop rationalizing that enthusiastic spurts are good enough given all the challenges you face. As Edward B. Butler voiced, "One man has enthusiasm for 30 minutes, another for 30 days, but it is the man who has it for 30 years who makes a success of his life."

Having made the commitment to being an energetic spirit, engage with things you totally believe in. Remember it's futile to try and muster excitement about things you don't believe in. You'll never give one hundred percent effort to something you don't believe in. Any effort to manufacture enthusiasm for things riddled with your doubts will be doomed to failure.

It is not hard for me to generate enthusiasm for life insurance. I have a strong belief in life insurance and for good reason. My father died prematurely at fifty years of age. His death was sudden and no one was prepared. In my previous book, *Go and Be Successful*, I tell the story of going into the bank the day following my dad's death. My parents had bought their first house later in life and there had been very little principle paid off the loan when this family tragedy happened. I was hoping that there was some insurance connected with the home loan. The bank manager regretfully informed me that there was no insurance connected to the mortgage documents and that, despite the sadness of my father's demise, the home mortgage payment was still due.

Fearing the prospects of losing the family home, I scoured my dad's office for anything that resembled a life insurance policy. For hours I searched through file upon file until I came across some paperwork that had the words 'Provident Fund' on it. I phoned the number on the document. A gentleman answered and quickly confirmed that the document I was holding was indeed a life insurance policy. His kindness was reassuring. He divulged the dollar amount of the coverage and finished the conversation by saying he was going to issue a check for the proceeds immediately. The relief that washed over me as I hung up the phone was incredible. I broke the news to my mother that the proceeds of the policy would be enough to save the family home. That's why it is not hard for me to garner enthusiasm for life insurance. I whole-heartedly believe in the premise of life insurance because my family was once rescued by it.

If you have a strong belief in something, generating enthusiasm for it will be easy. If you believe that the future is bright, generating enthusiasm about the future will naturally flow. If you are struggling to have an upbeat spirit, it is likely that you have lost connection with the things that you believe in, or worse, you have simply stopped believing.

Know your business and be an expert in it. To thoroughly understand your product and its benefits will help you to believe in it. Once you believe in it, you can get enthusiastic about it. If you don't believe in your service or product, any manufactured enthusiasm about it will be short lived and unconvincing.

Maximize the Effectiveness of Your Enthusiasm

Your enthusiasm will open more doors by letting someone else profit from it. Mr. Clifford taught me this early in my career. I was working hard to get his business and he had shown some promising initial interest. However, translating his interest into any bankable business was proving difficult. I was enthusiastic alright, enthusiastic to benefit from Mr. Clifford's business. Out of frustration for the lack of advancement, I decided to get on a plane and take Mr. Clifford out to lunch. It was a big investment but I hoped that meeting with him personally would cause a breakthrough.

When the day came for the meeting, I carefully selected my business suit, tie, and shoes. I wanted to make an outstanding first impression. When I got off the plane, Mr. Clifford met me wearing his tennis gear. Boy, did I feel foolish being so overdressed. I hoped we would go to a dimly lit restaurant. No luck. Mr. Clifford took me to the airport food court, just one step up from a vending machine! I sensed that I was an interruption to his tennis match and that he wanted to get lunch over with quickly.

Having finished lunch, Mr. Clifford looked at me and asked, "Well, what can I do for you?" This was my moment. I immediately thought, 'Wes, what are you waiting for? He just offered to help you. Ask him for his business!' But it just didn't seem the right thing to do. I looked at Mr. Clifford and saw a man with the weight of a huge organization on his shoulders. I figured the last thing he needed was another person hitting him up for his help. I determined right then to forget about my needs and concentrate on his needs. Turning the table, I asked if there was any way I could help him.

We talked together for a considerable time. I came to understand Mr. Clifford's needs and what I could do to benefit his bottom line. I knew to proceed, however, would make no difference to my bottom line. In the following weeks, I helped Mr. Clifford on a special project. The outcome was to his sole benefit. I would go home without any payment for my services.

A few months later the phone rang. It was Mr. Clifford. He asked me to help him on another project. Then his colleagues started calling. Invitations for my services began to flow and so did the money. Big money. Fourteen years later, I am still getting well paid invitations that I can trace back to meeting Mr. Clifford in the airport food court.

The doors of opportunity started to open when I changed from being enthusiastic about meeting my needs to being enthusiastic about meeting someone else's needs.

Often the best way to release the power of enthusiasm in your life is to let someone else get the benefit of your enthusiasm.

The bottom line is that enthusiasm fuels success. Whatever the problem may be, the answer begins with your enthusiasm.

———

Now to the How To: Enthusiasm

1. Don't wait for the right conditions. Make a personal commitment to being an enthusiastic person.

2. Learn the benefits of your product or service to intensify your belief in them.

3. Show enthusiasm not only for your own needs but for the needs of others. Lend your enthusiasm towards the fulfillment of someone else's goal.

4. Accept that life is a waveform of ups and downs. Don't let the 'downs' steal your enthusiasm. Use your enthusiastic disposition to change your conditions.

Quick Fuel: Enthusiasm

If you are not getting as much from life as you want to, then examine the state of your enthusiasm.
Norman Vincent Peale

For every sale you miss because you're too enthusiastic, you will miss a hundred because you're not enthusiastic enough. *Zig Ziglar*

Enthusiasm releases the drive to carry you over obstacles and adds significance to all you do. *Norman Vincent Peale*

None are so old as those who have outlived enthusiasm. *Henry David Thoreau*

Enthusiasm. . . the sustaining power of all great action. *Samuel Smiles*

I found that the men and women who got to the top were those who did the jobs they had in hand, with everything they had of energy and enthusiasm and hard work. *Harry S. Truman*

A man can succeed at almost anything for which he has unlimited enthusiasm. *Charles M. Schwab*

A salesman minus enthusiasm is just a clerk. *Harry F. Banks*

Nobody grows old merely by living a number of years. We grow old by deserting our ideals. Years may wrinkle the skin, but to give up enthusiasm wrinkles the soul. *Samuel Ullman*

Be enthusiastic as a leader. You can't light a fire with a wet match! *Unknown*

Success Workshop: Enthusiasm

1. On the following scale, how would you rate your reputation for being enthusiastic?

Low   High

2. Does enthusiasm come more easily to you in some situations and not in others? When you become enthusiastic what triggers that enthusiasm?

_____

_____

3. Name three people in your life that inspire you with their enthusiasm? How do they express their enthusiasm?

_____

_____

4. Can you recall a time when your lack of enthusiasm cost you an opportunity?

_____

5. Describe a situation that would greatly benefit from more of your enthusiasm.

_____

_____

6. What behavior are you prepared to change in order to establish a reputation for being enthusiastic?

_____

F. Focus

If you're going to hunt elephants,
don't get off the trail for a rabbit.
T. Boone Pickens

———◦◦◦———

Distractions are enemy number one for anyone with a goal. Staying focused is the biggest challenge for any motivated person. By nature we are prone to being distracted. That's why shopping malls are so effective. Someone figured out that if many stores formed a cluster, then sales for all stores would go up. You may go to a shopping mall to buy some new shoes and come home with two shirts, a coat, some blue jeans, and some candles. Then upon returning home, you realize that you have to go back to the mall the next day because you never got around to buying those shoes! I hear women saying, "Hey, I didn't get distracted. Those items were on sale!" Indeed those items were a bargain but they were put on sale to distract you. To be fair, send a guy to buy a toaster and he's just as likely to come home with a flat screen TV!

Sometimes I envy people who are extraordinarily talented at one thing. Demand for their 'one thing' keeps them focused on their one thing. For the rest of us, we have an all around reasonable level of competence for many tasks. It's sometimes referred to as being 'cursed with competence.' Why cursed? Because we can end up doing countless things, being pulled in all directions, heading in no particular direction.

Success comes when you choose one goal and fight a daily war against everything that would divert your attention from your progression towards that goal. Anything not directly associated with the achievement of your objective, no matter how noble, will delay your arrival. Focus is the most fuel efficient way to get to your desired goal. Focus transforms life from being an overwhelming blur of possibilities to being a confident pathway to the fulfillment of your purpose.

The Anatomy of Focus

Focus is gathering your resources, as an army general would assemble his soldiers, and concentrating them to such potency upon a goal that it surrenders at your charge. Focus is the ability to look at a world of options and, forsaking all others, marry one, and re-marry that one every day! Focus requires intolerance to distractions, no matter how noble. Many a person has been robbed of their life purpose because they kept stopping to serve innocent distractions.

The natural tendency of life is towards the dilution of our potential. If you were to put a drop of ink on your palm, you would carry the stain for days. Put that same drop of ink in a river and it would dilute and be gone in seconds. Life will naturally dilute your powers and resources. By focus, you concentrate all your powers and resources to become a potent force in the attainment of your goals. You cannot succeed by accident. It will be the result of your commitment to focus your energies and stop them from being diluted. Focus essentially fuels you to succeed.

The Formation of Focus

Economist Ben Stein says, "The indispensable first step to getting the things you want out of life is this: decide what you want." How sweet it is to finally know what you specifically want in life. We all know what it's like to chase two rabbits and to come home empty handed. Knowing what you want and then applying full concentration towards attaining it is the best way to avoid coming home empty handed.

Forget trying to be focused if your goal isn't clearly defined. If I were to throw ten ping pong balls to you all at once, commanding you to catch the best one, you would battle with indecision. You would wonder, "Which one is the 'best' one?" Now, if one of those ping-pong balls was painted blue and you were instructed to catch the blue one, it would be easier. You would focus completely on the blue ball and mentally block out the rest as if they didn't exist. None of your energy would be lost to indecision and uncertainty. All of your energy would be concentrated on catching that blue ball. When it comes to getting ahead in life, you need to evaluate all of your goals and paint one of them blue.

One Goal – One Focus

In the 1600's, French Philosopher Blaise Pascal wrote, "However vast a man's spiritual resources, he is capable of but one great passion." Many people lament not being able to focus. But a 'lack of focus' is often not the problem. Not having a 'clear' goal is their problem. They have too many goals. Having too many goals is just as bad as having no goal. An abundance of targets blurs them all.

Every goal requires you to position yourself in a certain way. Having too many goals puts you in the predicament of not knowing how to position yourself. You keep changing your posture to suit whichever of your many goals happens to be attracting your attention at that time. As George S. Patton once said, "No good decision was ever made in a swivel chair."

To make focusing easier, you need to choose one goal. I repeat, one goal. That's where people get stuck. They are not sure which the 'best' goal is for them. So they put many goals on the soccer field of life and just start kicking balls in all directions hoping that whatever goal nets the most balls is the best goal.

There is a problem with this multi-goal approach. Keep it up for long enough and you'll end up with a few balls in every goal, still not sure which is the best one. So you continue running around the field madly kicking in all directions, not sure whether you are winning the game or just getting tired. Moderate success in a multiplicity of directions will leave you more confused than confident about what you are doing with your life.

Stop the multi-goal juggle. Choose one goal and make it number one. Even if all your goals have merit, to be effective in life you ultimately have to choose one goal and eliminate the others from the field. Then with singular focus, posture everything about yourself towards getting the ball up the field and into that goal.

A Goal That Makes You Want to Focus

Whatever goal you choose, it has to excite you. It has to be something that you really want and are willing to sacrifice to have. It must so invigorate your senses that you want to focus. A 'mediocre' goal won't have the inspirational thrust to keep you going. A goal that requires average ambition will only have enough inspirational fuel to get you through one or two rough patches before you give up completely. So whittle your goal list down to one. Make it a big elephant-sized aspiration and not one the size of a rabbit.

Having one goal, an audaciously inspiring one, with all your energies harnessed in pursuit of it, is the most effective way to succeed. As Zig Ziglar says, "I don't care how much power, brilliance or energy you have, if you don't harness it and focus it on a specific target, and hold it there, you're never going to accomplish as much as your ability warrants."

Quit Getting Distracted

Life is like a shopping mall, full of tempting opportunities to become diverted from your goal. Quit getting distracted. And if you do, then never let your distractions take over. Be your own distraction police. If you start swerving out of your lane, remind yourself that you are getting off track. Daily re-commit to your goal. If something is jockeying for your loyalties, remind yourself that you are already married to an objective.

According to Lou Holtz, "All winning teams are goal-oriented. Teams like these win consistently because everyone connected with them concentrates on specific objectives. They go about their business with blinders on; nothing will distract them from achieving their aims." Sometimes you need blinders on to avoid being distracted. In this way, you can maintain a steady, unswerving focus. There is a lot of fuel in being singularly focused and you will benefit from every drop in your journey to the top.

—◦/◦/◦—

Now to the How To: Focus

1. Decide what you want. Determine what is your number one goal.

2. Set all other goals aside for now and focus all your energies on your one goal.

3. Make a list of common distractions. Determine which of those distractions are entirely unnecessary and stop entertaining them.

4. Make a daily commitment to focus on goal #1 and do not get distracted.

Quick Fuel: Focus

Realize what you really want. It stops you from chasing butterflies and puts you to work digging gold.
William Moulton Marston

Most people have no idea of the giant capacity we can immediately command when we focus all of our resources on mastering a single area of our lives. *Anthony Robbins*

It is those who concentrate on but one thing at a time who advance in this world. The great man or woman is the one who never steps outside his or her specialty or foolishly dissipates his or her individuality. *Og Mandino*

The single universal quality among every successful person I know is they all have an incredibly high level of energy focused on one thing. *Jay Chiat*

No steam or gas drives anything until it is confined. No life ever grows great until it is focused, dedicated, disciplined. *Harry Emerson Fosdick*

If you want to be truly successful invest in yourself to get the knowledge you need to find your unique factor. When you find it and focus on it and persevere your success will blossom. *Sidney Madwed*

The immature mind hops from one thing to another; the mature mind seeks to follow through. *Harry A. Overstreet*

Without goals, you will end up going nowhere, or, you will end up following someone else's map! Develop your map today—set your goals and focus! *Catherine Pulsifer*

Concentration is the key to economic results. No other principles of effectiveness is violated as constantly today as the basic principle of concentration. *Peter F. Drucker*

I never could have done what I have done without the habits of punctuality, order, and diligence, without the determination to concentrate myself on one subject at a time. *Charles Dickens*

Success Workshop: Focus

1. On the following scale, how easy is it for you to focus?

Hard   Easy

2. Do you have a clearly defined #1 goal? What is it?

_____

_____

3. What are three of your biggest distractions?

_____

_____

_____

4. What have you achieved in the past as a result of being forced to focus? What are some ways that you can force yourself to focus?

_____

_____

_____

5. What benefits would you experience as a result of achieving your #1 goal? Would the benefits be sufficient enough reward for your discipline?

_____

_____

_____

_____

2

Reading

2. Reading

How many a man has dated a new era in his life
from the reading of a book.
Henry David Thoreau

━━━━◦◦◦━━━━

It was Albert Einstein who said, "You cannot solve
a problem with the same mind that created it." The key to
solving your problems is to tackle them with a transformed mind. The best way to transform your mind is to
read books that raise the level of your thinking. And read
them every day.

The invention of the printing press has liberated
mankind more than any war. Books have been the avenue
of escape for every person wanting to de-shackle themselves from their present limitations. That is why every
political regime bent on removing people's freedoms,
starts with the banning and burning of books. In order to
curtail a person's ambitions, you must deny their access to
material that would fuel those ambitions.

Through the written word we gain access to the
great minds that have gone before us, what they learned,
what they discovered, and how it can benefit us. We don't

have time to gain all our learning from making mistakes. Writers give us the opportunity to learn from theirs. Take a key from Socrates: "Employ your time in improving yourself by other men's writings so that you shall come easily by what others have labored hard for." Reading great books will give you the fuel to push through the inevitable headwinds between you and success.

Recently, I was at the local grocery store and could not help but overhear an impassioned customer giving the manager a sizeable portion of her displeasure. She had a legitimate issue. She had bought a gift card for a friend and was embarrassed when her friend returned the gift card saying it did not work. Apparently, something had gone wrong in the activation process when the card was purchased at the grocery store. I could not fault the lady for being angry. What was meant to bring joy and happiness to a friend became a source of embarrassment and another problem to solve.

Try as the customer did to escalate the problem into a national disaster, the store manager respectfully brought her back to a center of calmness each time he was given a chance to respond. He exhibited tremendous control in the heat of a delicate situation. Customers and staff were all around him. Everyone could hear. Yet, he didn't look the least bit uncomfortable or intimidated by her outbursts. Ultimately the manager was able to defuse the crisis without 'giving her the store' just to calm her down.

When I had completed my shopping, I asked if I could talk to the same store manager. As he walked towards me, I wondered whether he was bracing himself for another challenge. I introduced myself and complimented him on his superb people skills. He confessed it had been quite a turbulent morning with customers and was quite relieved and grateful to hear some good news. I asked how he had remained so composed and respectful of the customer even when she was ripping shreds off him. He replied, "I have been reading a book about 'getting to the core issues'. It has really changed my life in how I deal with people."

Surely, whatever that book cost was well worth it. I am convinced that in the hands of that store manager, it was saving the store from losing thousands of dollars in future business.

Make It a Daily Commitment

It's unfortunate that the term 'brainwashing' was given to the cult world as a description of their mind control techniques. I think of brainwashing differently. With the junk that our brain has to filter, it certainly needs a good cleaning regularly. I wear my favorite pair of jeans all of the time. Yet, there comes a day when I have to throw those jeans in the wash. Through constant wear, they become soiled and unattractive. Washing them forces the foreign matter out and the clean freshness in! Reading books has the same impact on our minds. Our brains are bombarded with information all day long. Some of this information puts the stink in the way we think. Reading positive and educational books flushes the mind of erroneous thinking and replaces it with constructive thinking. The mind is destined to become stale, jaded, and uninspired if not continually refreshed with new thoughts.

I always struggled with reading books. Perhaps the struggle was more in finding time to actually read. Either way, on May 15th, 1981 that all changed. I met a man named Gary Speckman. I spent a few hours with him and have never seen him since. Yet in those few hours Gary inspired me to read in a way that turned me into an avid reader and ultimately, an author.

After a short time of being with me, he diagnosed that my lack of vitality was largely due to my stale thinking. He challenged me to read more and refused to accept any of my lame excuses. He proceeded to give me his sixty day challenge. The crux of the challenge was to spend twenty minutes a day reading something inspirational and then writing my response to it in a journal. At the time, I was more interested in proving myself capable of meeting the challenge than actually reading. The caveat to the challenge was that I had to do it for sixty consecutive days. If for any reason I missed a day, I had to go back to the beginning and start over.

It was quite a challenge. Some days I would jump into bed only to realize I had not fulfilled my reading commitment. So I would climb back out of bed to read and write about it in my journal. Frankly, sometimes what I read wasn't worth climbing out of bed for! Other times what I read would completely change my demeanor. The commitment to achieving sixty consecutive days kept me reading regardless of what I gained from it. Yet, over the sixty days, I could sense my mind being transformed.

I finally succeeded in reaching the sixty day mark without missing a day. The impact that reading positive material every day had on my life was undeniable. So I decided to incorporate the practice into my daily life from that point onwards. Twenty-seven years later, I am still taking twenty minutes every day to read something inspiring and educational. It is my daily brain-washing. Without a doubt, reading a few pages each day from a positive instructional book has been a major influencing factor of my success.

Some people give up on reading because they say they can't remember what they read a few days later. Don't worry about it. I don't remember a single meal I ate last week, but it doesn't mean I am going to stop eating! The key to remember is that what you read today will sustain and influence your day. Over time, you'll be surprised how much of what you read seeps into your mind and changes your life. Make the commitment to read every day.

Reading Increases Your Focus Ability

Some people can't focus because the part of their brain that helps them focus has atrophied from non-use. The advent of television, computers, and other visual-stimulant media is largely to blame. People tend to lose interest in something that is not presented in a visually stimulating format. Pediatrician Dr. Jane Healy writes, "The compellingly visual nature of [media] stimulus blocks development of left-hemisphere language circuitry. A young brain manipulated by jazzy visual effects cannot divide attention to listen carefully to language. Moreover, the 'two-minute mind' easily becomes impatient with any material requiring depth of processing."

The person who trains themselves to be a reader gains an absolute competitive advantage over non-readers. Readers become more successful, not only because of the information they read but because the process of reading develops an important part of brain function. Neil Postman, author of *Amusing Ourselves to Death*, points out that, "Reading teaches us to think in logically connected ways.

It cultivates a sustained attention span. Readers learn to think in terms of abstract ideas, objective truth, and sustained reflection. When this is replaced with graphic imagery, like television (especially commercials) and movies, there is a tendency toward shorter attention spans and a purely emotional response to what is offered. Once addicted to graphical stimulation, there is an increased demand for constant, entertaining stimulation that can hinder the capacity for delayed gratification."

If there is any road that requires depth of processing or navigational capacities, it is the road to success. Reading expands the part of your brain that helps you navigate obstacles and normalize difficulty. Those who need constant stimuli to keep interested will find any opportunity objectionable which is not served to them already baked complete with frosting. They are so conditioned to having all the thinking done for them that their ability to process challenges is undeveloped. Every difficulty becomes an impossible situation because they lack the ability to analyze it and develop an unemotional strategy to overcome it. With the expansion of their brain processing function by reading, readers become endowed with a superior ability to normalize challenges and deal with them in a less emotional way.

If you are a leader of a team, take note of this. Get your people reading, not just for the content but to expand the processing part of their brains. Readers will less likely need your attention as challenges arise. Their developed capacity to process issues serves them in such times. What others see as severe problems, readers will 'normalize' as par for the course.

Double the Value of Reading By Writing About It

The practice of writing my response to what I read helped me to personalize the content and make it real to my life. David Schwartz once said, "When you write on paper, you write it on your mind too." Writing about what you read forces you to process its relevance to your life. As my friend, Charlie 'Tremendous' Jones, would say, "Always read with a pen in your hand. Cultivate the habit of making notes of things you actually think in addition to what you thought you read." Writing your personal response to what you read will double the life changing impact of what you read.

Re-write Your Future by Reading What was Written in the Past

Recently the world lost a treasure in the passing of Charlie 'Tremendous' Jones. He was a giant of a man in so many ways. His life was dedicated to getting people to read inspirational books. He was always saying, "You will be the same in five years as you are today except for the books you read and the people you meet."

I remember the time that Charlie was coming to speak to my leadership team. I picked him up from San Diego and had two incredible hours of time with him as we drove to Los Angeles. I peppered Charlie with questions and he would excitedly read to me sections from books that he was currently reading. That night, with the energy of a teenager, Charlie 'Tremendous' Jones spoke to a room packed full of leaders. I was amazed to see this man in his eighties absolutely on fire with passion for life. It was not hard to see that books fueled Charlie's passion for life and zeal for people.

I love books both for their information and the expanding effect that they have on my capacity to process my way forward. Reading fills your fuel tank with energy to succeed.

———⟋⟋⟋———

Now to the How To: Reading

1. If you are not a natural book buyer, join a monthly business book program.

2. Commit to reading twenty minutes a day for personal growth.

3. Keep a journal and write a daily paragraph of your reflections on what you read.

4. Encourage growth in your friends and family by giving them great books to read.

5. Find a reading partner or form a reading group to read and discuss books together.

6. Listen to audio books in your car or when you go out for walks.

Quick Fuel: Reading

Some people will lie, cheat, steal and back-stab to get ahead. . . and to think, all they have to do is READ. *Fortune*

Reading is to the mind what exercise is to the body. *Sir Richard Steele*

Life-transforming ideas have always come to me through books. *Bell Hooks*

We read to know we are not alone. *C.S. Lewis*

Reading is a means of thinking with another person's mind; it forces you to stretch your own. *Charles Scribner, Jr.*

When you sell a man a book you don't sell him just 12 ounces of paper and ink and glue—you sell him a whole new life. *Christopher Morley*

No matter how busy you may think you are, you must find time for reading, or surrender yourself to self-chosen ignorance. *Confucius*

Books are the quietest and most constant of friends; they are the most accessible and wisest of counselors, and the most patient of teachers. *Charles W. Eliot*

When I get a little money, I buy books; and if any is left, I buy food and clothes. *Desiderius Erasmus*

Today a reader, tomorrow a leader. *Margaret Fuller*

Success Workshop: Reading

1. Name three books that have transformed your life. What did you like about them?

_____

_____

_____

_____

_____

2. What time of day is best for you to read? Where do you like to go to read?

_____

_____

3. What is the advantage in reading books that may differ from your opinion?

_____

_____

4. Do you have a particular book that you keep going back to re-read? Why?

_____

_____

5. What changes can you make in your life to create more time for reading?

_____

_____

3

Resources

3. Resources

He that waits upon fortune, is never sure of a dinner.
Benjamin Franklin

———⌐⌐⌐———

If you lost your job, how much income would continue to flow into your life on a weekly basis? For most of the population the answer would be none. What's worse the bills would continue to roll in, irrespective. To have costs but not have the resources to cover them brings tremendous stress to individuals and families. A lack of financial resources is the number one cause of marriage stress today. On the other hand, most economic stress is completely annihilated when you have cash resources set aside. Without having cash resources, every economic wind becomes a veritable storm that keeps you anxiously awake at night. You will feel much stronger when you have some 'storm funds' socked away.

Money is one of the keys to happiness. It is rare to find a person insolvent and happy. The people that I know trying to make it on an empty financial fuel tank are highly stressed and do not sleep well. The sentiment of 'being content with what you have' is really tested when you can't afford to take your child to the doctor. With due respect to the perils of greed, let us not overlook the reality that poverty is not exactly a blessing. Without money, your options are vastly limited, including being able to help the poor. I have experienced life at both ends and while I respect how insolvency deepens one's character, insolvency is still a place better visited than a place permanently lived.

From my experience and observing those besieged by a lack of money, not having the financial resources to effectively meet your needs literally drains the life out of you. Insolvency is like living with holes in your fuel tank. Precious energy is lost worrying instead of being utilized in being creative and productive. Personal confidence plummets when your bank account is empty. A dire financial condition impairs people's judgment and often leads them to making irrational decisions that lead to painful consequences.

Your Personal Economic Policy

Having said all of the above, more money in the hands of people is not necessarily the solution. More money in the hands of those without an economic plan is only a temporary reprieve. A bailout without a corresponding change of financial behavior just buys a little more time before the need for another bailout. Often people find themselves poor because of inadequate life planning.

A lack of cash is symptomatic of a lack of money management. The financial answer for everyone lies in establishing a personal economic plan. If you develop a sense of urgency to establish an economic plan now, it will save you from experiencing an emergency to find money later. Too often people wait until they are in a financial pickle before they consider establishing a plan. By then it's too late because a plan needs the benefit of time to work. It's too late to build a shelter once the storm is upon you.

Don't get led astray with arguments about 'How much is enough?' It's the management of our resources that liberates us rather than the amount of our resources. In the words of Edmund Burke, "If we command our wealth, we shall be rich and free. If our wealth commands us, we are poor indeed." It is an issue of command not the amount. Money is morally neutral. It is in the control or lack of control that gives money its moral definition. If the love of money is the root of all evil, so can be the lack of it. Don't think for one moment that 'not' having money frees you from the perils of wealth. An envious, poor person is at moral risk just as much as the proud, prosperous one. The world desperately needs people who know how to command money, regardless of the amount, and not have it command them.

Substantive resources are shock absorbers in the journey of life. Financial reserves absorb much of the effects of hitting the inevitable bumps in the road. Without resources, you will feel every financial pothole you encounter. If you haven't got spare resources to absorb the impacts, your senses become so jarred that making prudent decisions becomes unlikely. Being well resourced affords you time to consider what decisions will lead to the best of outcomes. That's one of the reasons why the rich keep getting richer—they are not rattled when the economy gets rough. They have the time to evaluate opportunities and go with the best one. Those without resources often don't have the time, confidence, or wherewithal to pursue the best opportunities.

If you aren't flushed with reserves, don't despair. The secret to a life of financial freedom is found in the management of your resources not the amount of your resources. The goal is to have the resources to meet all your situations effectively. That is an equilibrium that can be experienced at any financial level. It comes down to effective money management. It starts with building up a healthy reserve.

Create 'Spread'

First and foremost, set a personal goal of having a sizeable cash reserve fund. Start with the aim to have one month's living expenses saved. Succeed in that and then press on to create six to twelve months of living expenses in cash savings. This will fuel your confidence to a whole new level. Achieve this by managing your lifestyle to fit well within your current income.

Too many people let their wants and desires, with the help of a few credit cards, set their lifestyle. The first step to becoming well resourced is to stop going backwards into debt and to start to live within your means. As I wrote in my book *Escape to Prosperity*, "To enter the world of prosperity, you must have a good earning to spending ratio. If you can keep a portion of what you earn and invest it, then wealth is on its way. If you spend all that you make, you will never be prosperous. It is not how much you make but how little of it you spend that is important."

Drive your expenses down and increase your income. Create 'positive spread'—the difference between your expenses and your income. For example if your expenses are eight gold coins a week and your income is ten gold coins a week, you have a positive spread of two gold coins a week. Take that positive spread, in other words your excess funds, and split it. Use half of it to pay down consumer debt and the other half put it in an interest bearing bank account. Keep it liquid. Don't play with it. For goodness sake, don't put it in a brokerage fund and try to trade stocks to get a better return on your money. Spending your time trying to outwit the stock market is a massive diversion from your main purpose. Your reserve fund is to release you from worry not to be a source of complication.

Once you have your financial ship stabilized with good reserves, then set your course to becoming wealthy by doing the following: keep increasing your income, work your business, continue to be ruthless with your expenses by paying off your debt, and stop non-essential services. With an increased spread, put it towards creating non-personal exertion income. That is income that you don't have to physically work for. As I like to describe it, "Income that turns up even when you don't."

Non-personal exertion income is the money that would continue to flow into your life, even if you stopped going to work. The primary forms of non-personal exertion income are business bonuses and residuals, dividends from share funds and bonds, rental income from real estate, and interest from cash assets. Investments that produce non-personal exertion income are required to meet my strict criteria. They must be low maintenance, free up my time rather than take up my time, and not be so complicated that I am enslaved to 'professionals' to understand and manage them.

There is so much benefit to having non-personal exertion income. Don't for one moment think that you lack the ability to create non-personal exertion income streams. You have as much potential as anyone. There is a fulfilling dimension to your confidence that will reveal itself when non-personal exertion income starts to flow to you. It increases your energy to face the world and have a greater impact in the world.

My Uncle Tom was a senior pilot with a major international commercial airline. He flew Boeing 747 jumbo jets and loved doing so. It was a sad day when, in his fifties, he reached the mandatory retirement age. With a love for aviation still in his heart, he found a way to keep utilizing his flying skills. Uncle Tom bought a Mitsubishi MU-2 turbojet and started flying to outer-lying regions of Australia on medical mercy flights. He picks up patients too sick to make long road trips over rugged terrain and flies them to medical treatment centers.

Apart from the scope of his flights, there are two aspects to Uncle Tom that inspire me. First, he is 74 years of age and still flying patients for emergency medical treatment. Second, the medical agency for whom he flies can only afford to cover 40% of the flight costs. Uncle Tom subsidizes the rest from his non-personal exertion income streams. Being well resourced gives Uncle Tom, literally, the fuel to succeed in making a big difference in the lives of others. Now that's what I'm talking about. Money buying happiness!

Command your resources, regardless of their size. Do all the right things: drive your expenses down, increase your income, create positive spread (excess funds), use your spread to pay off debts, buy a home, establish cash reserves, and build up non-personal exertion income investments. It is not a complicated process to build up your resources. The more you do, the more fuel you will have to advance to greater places in life. Money in the bank is fuel in your tank.

———⟨∞⟩———

Now to the How To: Resources

1. Determine how long you could survive if you lost your employment income today.

2. Set a specific financial goal for a reserve fund.

3. Start creating positive spread—the difference between how much money comes in and how much goes out. Negative spread would indicate that you have more money going out than coming in. Establish a healthy reserve fund.

4. If you are in a mess financially, don't worry (because we have all been there and worry is such a waste of energy!) Read any of Dave Ramsey's books to help you get your financial act together. You can also read my book called *Escape to Prosperity*.

5. Start creating non-personal exertion income streams.

Quick Fuel: Resources

Money isn't the most important thing in life, but it's reasonably close to oxygen on the 'gotta have it' scale. *Zig Ziglar*

Often we don't really need a miracle, we just need to develop better spending and saving habits. *Joel Osteen*

Be industrious and frugal, and you will be rich. You will, by such conduct, stand the best chance for such consequences. *Benjamin Franklin*

When opportunity comes, it's too late to prepare. *John Maxwell*

Money is neither my god nor my devil. It is a form of energy that tends to make us more of who we already are, whether it's greedy or loving. *Dan Millman*

Wealth is power. With wealth many things are possible. *George Clason*

Becoming wealthy is not a matter of how much you earn, who your parents are, or what you do. . . it is a matter of managing your money properly. *Noel Whittaker*

It frees you from doing things you dislike. Since I dislike doing nearly everything, money is handy. *Groucho Marx*

We live by the Golden Rule. Those who have the gold make the rules. *Buzzie Bavasi*

Wealth is the product of man's capacity to think. *Ayn Rand*

Success Workshop: Resources

1. Do you consider yourself to be financially competent? Why or why not?

_____

_____

2. If you lost your employment income, how many months could you survive before financial catastrophe?

_____

3. Does the word 'budget' energize you or make you cringe? Why?

_____

_____

4. How many credit cards do you have active? Do you carry balances or pay them off each month?

_____

_____

5. What appeals to you the most: a) Having so much money that you don't need to keep track of your spending *or* b) Having millions but having a strong sense of command over what comes in and what goes out? Which is the better way to be?

_____

_____

_____

_____

4

Realizations

4. Realizations

You have power over your mind—not outside events.
Realize this, and you will find strength.
Marcus Aurelius

———⟨⊘⊘⊘⟩———

Realizing a profit begins with acting on your
realizations. A realization is that moment in time when all
your thoughts step aside to make way for one profound
thought. They are also known as epiphany moments. A
boy dates a girl and, at one moment in time, realizes he
wants to spend the rest of his life with her. Someone else
looks across the boardroom table to see his company
president in the grip of anxiety and, in that one moment,
realizes he is staring at his own future if he continues
down that career track. A dad dreams of taking his family
to Hawaii, but cutbacks in his workplace lead him to a
stark moment of awareness that his current job will never
provide enough to get his family there.

These are realization moments and they can be
the turning point in one's life if acted upon. These are
times when we awaken to a certain reality. Some of us
make radical changes, while others go right back to sleep.

Realizations are powerful in their ability to activate positive change. Be fueled by your realizations. These epiphany moments can be life changing if you take notice of them and let them propel you to make positive changes. Every successful person can attest to key moments of realization which they acted upon. It was acting upon their realizations that set them towards success.

1. Realize that your condition cannot improve until you stop blaming the conditions for your condition.

Even if you are the recipient of unfair treatment and misfortune, you will be imprisoned for as long as you give injustice the credit for your current condition. Albert Ellis said it well, "The best years of your life are the ones in which you decide your problems are your own. You do not blame them on your mother, the ecology, or the president. You realize that you control your own destiny."

To whomever you blame, you give the keys to your future. No one is worthy of that control. Your life goes to a new level of freedom and potential when you finally take full responsibility for your life. That moment when you look in the mirror and declare the words of James Allen over your life, "I am the architect—for better or worse—of my own future."

The benefits of blame are non-existent. Blame is often a way of covering some other malady such as a wounded mentality, a lack of drive, or disbelief in oneself. Plain laziness loves to dress up as a victim of circumstances. Realize that your condition can start to improve when you stop blaming the conditions for your condition. Wake up to this and let it fuel your advancement.

2. Realize that it is what you do and the conversations you have in your low times that will determine how soon you'll be back to the high times.

Life is a series of peaks and valleys. We can never eradicate all the valleys. Our goal at the end of each year should be, after throwing all our mountains and valleys into a box, come up with a higher average than the previous year's average. That result is called 'overall growth.' People's overall growth is very much influenced by what they do in their valleys. For those who sit on their circumstances waiting for a 'ski-lift' to take them back up the mountain, there will be more time in the valley. For those who get busy in the valley, there will be less 'valley time' and more mountain tops than their counterparts.

You can tell the potential success in a person by their activities and conversations in their low times. My friend, John Mason, recently said, "The faith that moves mountains always carries a pick." Engage yourself in the solution process. Success-oriented people combat tough times with action. It is not only the solution to getting back to good times, it also makes the tough time pass more quickly.

Cesare Pavese was noted saying, "One stops being a child when one realizes that telling one's trouble does not make it any better." When you are in the valley, you can reinforce the valley by talking about it. Or when you are in the valley, you can minimize the negative impact by talking about the joys of the coming mountain top.

Realize that the better the quality of your activities and conversations in your low times, the quicker you'll get back to high times.

3. Realize that you are better than you think.

This is a great realization at which to arrive. The only thing is that you have to go through pain to get there. Every person needs at least one massive failure in their life. It's the only way to truly discover that failure is not the death of you. Everyone underestimates what they can endure. It's not until you get to the other side of a trauma do you discover how tough you really are. Discovering your resilience does wonders for your self-respect.

Learn as much from the mistakes of others as you can. But don't avoid attempting great things for fear of not succeeding. In the words of Charles de Gaulle, "A man of character finds a special attractiveness in difficulty, since it is only by coming to grips with difficulty that he can realize his potentialities." So do not be afraid of difficulty. It is the great revealer of your resilience. Failure is never all bad when you discover, by surviving it, that you are stronger than you previously estimated.

My brother and businessman, Cameron, has these words inscribed as a reminder to every entrepreneur, "If you're insecure. . . relax! The rest of the world is as well. Do not overestimate the competition and underestimate yourself—you are better than you think."

4. Realize that no one is against you, they're just for themselves.

More and more, I am convinced that we become personally offended way too easily. We have a propensity to read into other people's response, or lack of response, a sense that they're disinterested or negative towards us.

The reality is that they are simply preoccupied with them-selves. We are all by nature giving most consideration to our own affairs.

Years ago when I was backpacking across Australia, I was having absolutely no luck in getting big rig trucks to stop and give me a ride. After about a hundred trucks had zoomed past on a lonely stretch of highway, I virtually wrote off truck drivers as self-serving renegades. Finally, one truck pulled over to the side of the road needing to fix something. I had nothing to lose so I asked him if he was open to me catching a ride. To my pleasant surprise, he was most obliging. He explained to me that once trucks get up to speed, they will rarely stop because they lose too much momentum and time in doing so. When the time came for him to drive in a different direction, he dropped me off at a truck stop and introduced me to another truck driver going in my direction.

So from one truck stop to another, I made my way from one side of Australia to the other. The last truck driver I asked for a ride was very grateful to take me. He had a fifty three foot 'long box' trailer full of carpet that needed to be at a retail store by eight o'clock in the morning. He had lost several hours due to a breakdown and meeting the delivery deadline meant he had to drive through the night. He informed me that my job was to keep him awake. I had a travel guitar with me, so I sang every song in my repertoire and repeated them several times!

In retrospect, my initial conclusion about truck drivers was wrong. They weren't self-serving. They weren't against helping out a backpacker. They were just very com-mitted to not losing their momentum and falling behind in their transit schedules. That first truck driver helped me to realize that.

Just because you are not getting a favorable response does not mean that people are against you, it's just they're fully engaged in their own lives. Turning yourself into a martyr and others into villains will do nothing to advance you, especially when it's not true. Finding ways to engage people at their points of need is what leads to win-win arrangements. Realizing this will put fuel in your tank.

5. Realize that the essentials are absolutely essential.

When our sons were young and giving Ellie and me grief with their behavior, we would banish them to what we called 'bedroom time.' To their bedrooms they would go until they 'found their happiness.' Their bedroom incarceration would only be for as long as it took for them to alter their attitude. Sometimes they would instantly discover their joy and be returned to civilian life quickly. Other times it would take them a few hours to find their happiness. Nonetheless, as soon as their attitudes reflected joy, life would suddenly become less restricted.

There are times when I notice my world has become smaller. It's usually the result of me losing one or more of the essential six. Losing any of my good attitudes, belief, confidence, drive, enthusiasm, and focus inevitably results in a feeling of restriction and containment. If I sense a spirit of limitation dominating my thoughts, I do a personal assessment on the essential six and ask what is missing. If I am lacking a good attitude, I will ask myself, "What will be the consequences of not having a good attitude?" If I am lacking confidence, I ask myself, "Will this confidence crisis help me succeed?"

Attitude, belief, confidence, drive, enthusiasm, and focus are more than just ideals to aim for. You will experience negative consequences for the absence of any one of these. They are not optional extras that you employ from time to time. Don't leave home without them and don't come home without them. Work all six qualities into your life and they will go to work for you.

Why are they essential? The answer is, because never will everything go right all of the time. The six essentials are your insurance policy against suffering the full effects of inevitable disappointments. William McFee once said, "Doing what's right is no guarantee against misfortune." Even if you are perfectly executing all things, the imperfect world can foil your efforts. Attitude, belief, confidence, drive, enthusiasm, and focus keeps you positioned for the best of outcomes in tough times and in good times. Realize that the six essentials are absolutely essential. Memorize them and daily recommit to them.

We come to significant realizations for a reason. Realizations are invitations to improve our journey. When you are woken up with a realization, don't go back to sleep. Let it empower you to a better performance. Let it change your ways. Realizing a profit always begins with capitalizing on the power within a realization.

⸺◦◦◦⸺

Now to the How To: Realizations

1. Stimulate realizations by reading, meeting with successful people, and going somewhere inspiring for the sole purpose of 'super-thinking.'

2. When a realization dawns on you, ask someone successful to weigh in on it to help you clarify it and profit from it.

3. Start a journal in which you can record your major life realizations. Develop a strategy for making the most of your realizations.

4. Ask successful people to tell you about their epiphany moments that profoundly changed their lives for the better.

Quick Fuel: Realizations

To overcome a fear, here's all you have to do: realize the fear is there, and do the action you fear anyway.
Peter McWilliams

Realize that when you get older, you either get senile or become gracious. There's no in-between. You become senile when you think the world short-changed you, or everybody wakes up to. . .[undermine] you. You become gracious when you realize that you have something the world needs, and people are happy to see you when you come into the room. *Carlos Santana*

In down times be thankful for your opportunities and don't expect to always be on the mountain top. When life goes up and down like a yo-yo it is flexibility that keeps us stabilized. *Fred Smith*

You may not realize it when it happens, but a kick in the teeth may be the best thing in the world for you. *Walt Disney*

People do not seem to realize that their opinion of the world is also a confession of character. *Ralph Waldo Emerson*

It all changed when I realized I'm not the only one on the planet who's scared. Everyone else is, too. *Stan Dale*

It's all in the decisions you make. Once you realize that, you can become happy. *James Holzier*

Count your blessings. Once you realize how valuable you are and how much you have going for you, the smiles will return, the sun will break out, the music will play, and you will finally be able to move forward the life that God intended for you with grace, strength, courage, and confidence. *Og Mandino*

Teaching is an instinctual art, mindful of potential, craving of realizations. *A. Bartlett Giamatti*

Many times a day I realize how much my own life is built upon the labors of my fellowmen, and how earnestly I must exert myself in order to give in return as much as I have received. *Albert Einstein*

Success Workshop: Realizations

1. Have you ever had an epiphany moment that radically changed your life?

_____

_____

_____

2. What personal realization has changed your life the most? Has there ever been a realization that you wished you had acted on?

_____

_____

_____

_____

3. Is there any place that you go such as the mountains, the beach, or conferences that stimulates realizations? Why do these places inspire your super-thinking?

_____

_____

_____

_____

4. What can you change in your routine to stimulate more life changing realizations?

_____

_____

5

Relationships

5. Relationships

Personal relationships are the fertile soil
from which all advancement, all success,
all achievement in real life grows.

Ben Stein

—⟨∅∅∅⟩—

The point of origin for most every success can be traced back to a pivotal relationship. While it is important to have a strong money bank, it's even more important to have a strong people bank. The direction of our lives is extremely influenced by our relationships. The flightpath to our future is determined by our relationships.

If you want to improve your life, change your lineup of associations. Have the courage to drop out of tired and destructive relationships. Have the courage to pursue relationships with inspiring people. Admittedly, that is easier said than done. Some tired relationships may not want to release you and high quality people aren't easily accessible. Regardless of the foibles of relational dynamics, an improved future demands addressing one's relational lineup. Great relationships are premium fuel to anyone wanting to excel. You must bid farewell to some people and work hard to enter the lives of others.

Life Relationships & Seasonal Relationships

Some relationships are for life. The rest are for seasons. Know the difference. Invest in your life relationships and transition your seasonal relationships. Seasonal relationships have a 'shelf life' of mutual benefit and then they end. Over time, some of your seasonal relationships may become life relationships but not all of them.

View relationships like your wardrobe. Old clothes are eventually retired and replaced with new clothes. Unless you suddenly lose fifty pounds or win the lottery, it's unlikely that you would discard all your current clothes, replacing them with a complete wardrobe of new outfits. Seasonal relationships are dynamic. You don't stick with the same set for life. You will have a natural attrition of people out of your life leaving room for replacements. When that happens, you are not being disloyal.

People often feel guilty for not keeping up with everyone. Free people to move on and give yourself permission to do likewise. You are creating room in their life, as well as yours, for fresh associations and new mutually beneficial synergies. Don't be afraid to let people go. If the relationship has been positive for both parties, a spirit of friendship will remain as well as the possibility that you can spend another season together in the future.

Gaining Access to Premium People

As you seek positive relationships, don't leave it to chance. Be proactive in building quality people into your life. Be intentional about finding inspiring people. In my book, *Give Your Life a Success Makeover*, I address this topic of intentionally building relationships with these words: "Relationships are so key to advancement that unless we make changes to our relationships, we are going to remain exactly where we are . . . The best way to launch yourself into the next level is to connect with someone who is already living at the next level."

Your life will improve just by being in the presence of premium people. But gaining access to their lives is not easy. Successful people rarely have relational vacancies in their lives. A business owner friend of mine pays ten thousand dollars a year to gain access to a cluster of twelve peer mentors. He considers it a highly valuable investment. In this group of high-level achievers, he gains counsel and accountability of a standard that he would never get elsewhere. A group of masterminds doesn't come together by accident. There are costs involved. Be willing to pay a premium to gain access and time with premium people.

Another way to gain access to premium people is to bring value to their life. Sow your efforts into their fields, to benefit their harvest. Be willing to contribute on more than one occasion. You have to prove that you are not a gold-digger, only out for what you can get from the relationship. You cannot 'bait and switch' on a successful person. They can smell a manipulative spirit before it even walks in the room. They've already been 'worked over' a thousand times. Bring value to their life first and over time you will win their respect, trust, and business. As Anthony Robbins says, "Some of the biggest challenges in relationships come from the fact that most people enter a relationship in order to get something. They're trying to find someone who's going to make them feel good. In reality, the only way a relationship will last is if you see your relationship as a place that you go to give, and not a place that you go to take."

Work at succeeding in something noteworthy. Your successes will help open the door to high level people. String together some 'worth mentioning' achievements. Don't brag but don't be bashful either. High level people haven't got the time to play hide n seek with your qualities. You will be more successful in garnering time with someone if you bring something obvious to the table that they perceive as interesting and valuable.

Entry into higher level relationships takes genuineness, time, and a lot of creative effort. The greatest relationships often take years to foster. Don't be in a hurry and try to rush the development of relationships with excellent people. Establish trust with them before you ask for their help. Remember the best way to win someone's trust is to earn it by bringing increase to their life first. Then when the river does start to flow both ways, always leave more than what you take.

Expect Flaws in High Level People

You know that you are relationally mature when you have a healthy understanding that nobody is perfect. Get to know the person you revere the most and soon you'll discover their faults. Idealizing others sets you up for disappointment when you discover they too have flaws and that they are not the magic solution to your problems. High level people have just as many idiosyncrasies and will inevitably fail to live up to your expectations. Understand that what makes high level people great is their success despite their faults, not the absence of faults.

Quit looking for the perfect person with whom to establish the perfect relationship in the perfect setting.

When you discover your hero has faults, be encouraged. It means that you can become a high level person even with your faults. Perfection is not what makes high level people. Their ability to succeed despite their inadequacies is what you should be interested in and aspire to copy.

Develop the High Level Person in You

The high level person in you is developed by relationships from both directions—from people ahead of you and from people behind you. If you only engage people ahead of you, it will give you a false sense that you are 'bringing up the rear.' It will perpetuate a feeling that you are always the laggard striving to advance. But you are far from being on the bottom rung.

In the minds of many, you are a high level person. Mentoring people behind you helps you to realize that you have premium elements in your life. Investing strength into the lives of others helps you to value your own strengths. Emboldening those behind you develops leadership savvy within you. It increases your people skills, wisdom, and confidence which ultimately helps you interact with those ahead of you. Often your influence with those behind you opens the door for relationships with those ahead of you. In your efforts to connect with high level people, remember that being a high level person in the lives of others helps to make it happen.

———

Now to the How To: Relationships

1. Give yourself permission to change your roster of relationships.

2. Stop spending time with people who make you feel worth less.

3. Don't leave your relationships to chance; be proactive in establishing a strong people bank.

4. Make a list of high level people you want in your life. Figure out a plan to come under their influence.

5. Quit expecting perfection in others. Successful people are not perfect. Their ability to succeed despite their foibles, is the inspiration factor to focus on.

6. Make a list of people that look to you as a high level person. Mentor those people.

Quick Fuel: Relationships

Each relationship nurtures a strength or weakness within you. *Mike Murdock*

Eagles don't flock—you have to find them one at a time. *H. Ross Perot*

If you want to effectively help someone, don't eliminate their disappointments, teach them how to deal with them. *Stan Endicott*

Why do people persist in a dissatisfying relationship, unwilling either to work toward solutions or end it and move on? It's because they know changing will lead to the unknown, and most people believe that the unknown will be much more painful than what they're already experiencing." *Anthony Robbins*

Associate yourself with men of good quality if you esteem your own reputation; for 'tis better to be alone than in bad company. *George Washington*

Get out of your relationships comfort zone. The more broadly you connect with people, the greater your potential to influence and be positively influenced by others. *John C. Maxwell*

When dealing with people, remember you are not dealing with creatures of logic, but creatures of emotion. *Dale Carnegie*

Problems in relationship occur because each person is concentrating on what is missing in the other person. *Wayne Dyer*

Every person is a new door to a different world. *Unknown*

An argument is always about what has been made more important than the relationship. *Hugh Prather*

Success Workshop: Relationships

1. Do you actively manage your relationship roster or are your relationships more the product of chance?

_____

2. Are there people in your life that cause you to feel less valued? Why do you continue to keep them in your lineup of relationships? What way can you let them go without causing offense?

_____

_____

_____

_____

3. Are there people in your relationship lineup that are there because you actively pursued a relationship with them? Who are they?

_____

_____

4. What makes you feel apprehensive about seeking relationships with high level people?

_____

_____

5. How can you be influenced by high level relationships if you can't become friends with them personally?

_____

_____

6

Results

6. Results

Superhuman effort isn't worth a
damn unless it achieves results.
Sir Ernest Henry Shackleton
(Antarctic Explorer 1874-1922)

———⚬⚬⚬———

The purpose of this book boils down to you
attaining results. Good results. Great results. Massive
improvement to your life. Getting to a place well beyond
where you are now. Do not take too much comfort in the
sentiment that says, "It's what you become in the journey
that matters most." Too often this sentiment is used to
ameliorate the failure to achieve an objective. You need
results. Results play an integral part in the development
of who you are.

True, the greatest part of our character is forged in
the challenging times. But if all you have is challenging
times with no bankable rewards, you are not going to
feel too good about your journey. As Ken Blanchard says,
"People who produce good results feel good about themselves." Victory is an essential part of the character
building journey. There are parts of your character that

need victory in order to be developed. Without satisfying results, a part of you remains unformed. Void of results, you are left to philosophize about your journey, instead of celebrating it. Without satisfying results, you are constantly justifying your struggle. That is emotionally draining. On the other hand, nothing fills your energy tank like having tangible benefits to show for your efforts.

Results validate the effort. It's the harvest which validates the burying of good seed in the ground. It's the fruit that validates acres of featureless fruit trees. You may have a great attitude but without results that good attitude is going to be harder and harder to maintain. You may believe in yourself but your belief will tilt towards doubt if you don't get positive results. Your journey is not the goal. Your character is not the goal. Your goal is to get results and by those results, forge a vibrant and positive character. In all of your doing, get results! Results not only validate your effort but they give you the fuel to achieve greater things.

Psychological Oxygen

The human spirit needs the psychological oxygen that comes with victories. You are suffocated into a state of despondency if you go too long without a success. The energy needed to attain big results comes from having many smaller victories along the way. No one can keep going without being fueled by breakthroughs of some nature. If you have been slogging away for some time without being fruitful then wisdom demands that you reassess your approach. In the words of David Schwartz, "Stay with your goal and don't waiver from it one inch.

But don't beat your head against a wall. If you are not getting results, try a new approach." It is essential to your well being to experience fulfilling outcomes as a part of your journey.

Your relationships are a key factor in getting results. Being connected to the wrong people will hinder you from flourishing. Find a relational environment where winning is regularly experienced and celebrated. From that winning environment you will gain ideas and good advice. Never stay in a people setting that allows floundering to become a comfortable norm. The absence of any wins will ultimately dull your ambition and nullify your potential. In order to succeed you must connect with those who are succeeding. Anthony Robbins says, "If you want to be successful, find someone who has achieved the results you want. Copy what they do and you will achieve the same results."

Let Failure Plays its Role

There is a definite role that failure plays in the success process. To get the good results, you have to endure lots of failures. The founder of the Honda Corporation, Soichiro Honda noted, "Success represents the 1% of your work which results from the 99% that is called failure." Yes, success is often hidden in a haystack of failures. Don't be alarmed by failing because it is part of the success process. But be careful that you don't let failure overstep its boundaries. All failure and no successes will roll your spirit under a bus leaving you without enough psychological energy to get back up. If you find yourself depleted of any 'rebound' energy, you have let failure overstep its boundaries.

Part of the role of failure is that it can help you to refine your approach. Failure can drive you to find better relationships. Failure can motivate you to improve your skills. But too much failure can cause you to give up trying to advance altogether. Never allow failure to have the final say in how far you go. Too many people have let their failures dictate their destiny. Failures can refine you but don't let them define you. You are the sum of your results not your failures. So do everything you can to create a long list of positive results in your life. Results will keep you motivated.

Create a 'Results Momentum'

There was a season in my life when a specific entrepreneurial pursuit was not returning satisfying results. Frustration was making me more earnest but it wasn't making me more effective. I was becoming functionally fixated. Hyper-attention to the process wasn't helping. Indeed, it was contributing to my frustration. It had been a long time between victories and I was languishing for lack of psychological oxygen. I wasn't feeling great about myself and I knew that my current state was not going to contribute to my effectiveness.

Without giving up on my goal, I looked for things I could do to create a sense of achievement—small goals where the attainment was well within my control. Indeed there were some areas of my life that had become loose and overlooked. My daily walks had slipped off my daily agenda! I figured that regaining some fitness was well within my control. Doing so was a victory. In addition to that, I reworked my personal budget. I cut back on some expenditure which freed up some money that I could set aside on a weekly basis. I designated this cash to a new 'giving fund' to benefit specific people in desperate circumstances. It was another small victory. I started writing personal notes of encouragement to people I appreciated. This effort gave me a sense of victory.

All told there were many little victories that I managed to string together. None of them were worthy of a press release but cumulatively they restored confidence in my ability to achieve. I was thinking better about myself and emerged re-energized for my entreprencurial endeavors.

When you string together some smaller personal victories, you create momentum. These smaller victories can give you momentum to succeed on a larger scale. Stephen Covey wrote, "The best way to predict your future is to create it." By creating victories in your life, even if they're small, you influence the quality of your future. Running low on self-esteem is really just an indication that it's been a while since you've had a breakthrough. Don't let a dearth of results start to formulate pessimism towards your future. You need fuel. Create some small victories to give you a psychological upswing. Look for what you can do to make a positive difference in a short amount of time. Positive results, no matter how undersized, all add up to get you moving forward.

⸺◦⦿◦⸺

Now to the How To: Results

1. Change your ways if after a significant effort you fail to achieve meaningful results. Your life will never be satisfying in a results vacuum.

2. Never allow floundering to become the norm.

3. Counsel with those who are getting results and emulate their ways.

4. If you are in a results dearth, get a psychological upswing by creating a list of achievable objectives and fulfill them.

5. Celebrate the results of others. Jealousy subdues your initiative.

Quick Fuel: Results

There are two kinds of people in the world: those who make excuses and those who get results. An excuse person will find any excuse for why a job was not done, and a results person will find any reason why it can be done. Be a creator, not a reactor. *Alan Cohen*

Insanity: doing the same thing over and over again and expecting different results. *Albert Einstein*

Effective leadership is not about making speeches or being liked; leadership is defined by results not attributes.
Peter Drucker

The man who gets the most satisfactory results is not always the man with the most brilliant single mind, but rather the man who can best coordinate the brains and talents of his associates. *W. Alton Jones*

Success requires first expending ten units of effort to produce one unit of results. Your momentum will then produce ten units of results with each unit of effort. *Charles J. Givens*

There's a difference between interest and commitment. When you're interested in doing something, you do it only when circumstance permit. When you're committed to something, you accept no excuses, only results. *Art Turock*

Because its purpose is to create a customer, the business has two—and only two—functions: Marketing and Innovation. Marketing and Innovation produce results. All the rest are costs. *Peter Drucker*

In life, the first thing you must do is decide what you really want. Weigh the costs and the results. Are the results worthy of the costs? Then make up your mind completely and go after your goal with all your might. *Alfred A. Montapert*

Forget about style; worry about results. *Bobby Orr*

People of accomplishment have a special ability to develop intensity at the right time over the right issue. Only an amateur keeps jumping up and down like a cheerleader. Many hardworking people fail to accomplish much because they lack intensity at the meaningful time. *Fred Smith*

Success Workshop: Results

1. Finish this sentence: When I am not getting the results that I want, I usually. . .

_____

2. How much failure is too much? At what point should you evaluate a radical change in your approach?

_____

_____

3. When you have a win, is it better to celebrate or get straight back out there in hot pursuit of another win?

_____

4. How have your victories developed you as a person?

_____

_____

5. Name three things that you can do to give you an immediate psychological upswing.

_____

_____

_____

6. Name three things that will help you to create a results momentum.

_____

_____

_____

7

Rest

7. Rest

What is without periods of rest will not endure.
Ovid

—⊶∽∽⊷—

This chapter is not endorsing doing nothing if all you've been doing is nothing! The last thing I want to do is validate non-productivity. If your rest isn't flanked either side by your productivity, then it is not rest but idleness. In the context of great effort, rest is not only validated but deemed absolutely necessary to the effort process.

Sometimes doing nothing is the only thing that will replenish our fuel tanks. Most of us learn this the hard way. We run out of gas a few times before we discover that always being on the go is no guarantee that we'll get there any quicker. Don't wait until you burn out before you give yourself a break. Learn to rest as a matter of routine not as a matter of recovery.

In the event that oxygen masks are needed on a flight, the airline attendants tell parents with children to put on their mask first before their assisting children. It's advice that runs counter to parenting instincts which is to take care of the helpless kids first. Yet, there is a time when putting yourself first can be the most unselfish thing that you do. If your spirit is worn out, you will be of little benefit to anyone. You are more valuable to everyone when you have fuel in your tanks. Exhibiting the qualities of the essentials—attitude, belief, confidence, drive, enthusiasm, and focus—is much easier when you are not physically and mentally exhausted. In your life there will be seasons when the only fuel that will fill your tank is the fuel of rest.

My best times of accomplishment come off the back of a rejuvenating vacation. By vacation, I don't mean going on an exhausting trip. I mean taking a meaningful mental, physical, and geographical break from work. It's called 'planned nothing.' When planned right, rest becomes the place from which my most powerful creative energy comes. Yet organizing a rest is often the hardest part for me. It seems my whole life is spent organizing. If it's not organizing events, it will be organizing flights, schedules, business meetings, and organizing staff. I love the challenge of my work and the results when plans come together. When it comes to planning a rest, it can easily become just another event to organize and so it often gets put on my 'when I get around to it' list—that list that you never get around to dealing with!

If you want to succeed you have to realize that rest is not an option. You may save yourself some money by not taking a break but in the end it is false economy. You can tape your business card over the flashing 'low fuel' warning light but it's not going to stop you from running out of gas. Taking a break is primarily protection against life breaking you. And the good things of life can be just as crushing as the bad stuff if you don't get away from it. As David Schwartz noted, "Every outstanding religious leader in history spent much time in solitude away from the distractions of life—to do their super thinking." Rest can be a better investment in our productivity than continuing on with the work itself. Productivity is the result of the right mixture of exertion and relaxation.

When I Relax I Feel Guilty

When I first joined the working world, I worked in a bookstore. One of the books we sold was called, *When I Relax I Feel Guilty*. As a young man, I remember thinking it was a strange thought. Why would anyone feel guilty about relaxing? It is such a natural thing to do! Now, I realize that when you have sweated enough to fill a few swimming pools, taken on enormous responsibilities, and leveraged your life to your potential, relaxing does not come easy. Work naturally falls into place; rest has to be wrestled into place. When we finally do get away from it, we worry about the 'opportunity cost' of being momentarily out of the loop.

We must first realize that rest is not the enemy to productivity. Indeed it is a vital component of the productive process. You are not wasting valuable time by taking a break. If you are currently doing uninspiring work that provides an income but little else, temporarily getting away from it will clear your head and help you strategize a logical way out of an uninspiring work situation. If you have succeeded in positioning yourself in satisfying work, you still need to get away from it. As my wife reminds me, "If you love doing something, make sure you take regular breaks from it, or else you will stop loving it."

When you constantly have your nose close to the grindstone, you are less likely to evaluate whether there are more efficient ways of getting the job done. We tend to work to routines rather than to efficiencies. It's not until we take a break from the routine that we free our minds to think about issues of efficiency. You will find it much easier to create a 'not to do' list when you get far enough away from the grindstone so that you see the futility in some of your ways.

Far from a waste of time and opportunity, periods of rest can lead to a vast increase in productivity. Feeling guilty about taking a break is a waste of energy. Give yourself permission and re-educate yourself about the pivotal role that rest plays in helping you succeed.

Your Exertion/Relaxation Rhythm

The balance between exertion and relaxation varies for everyone. Find your rhythm. Don't wait until you have run out of gas before you start to address the need for a break. By then you will be too burned out to have the energy to do anything. Burnout strikes people in different ways. I used to think that burnout was getting to a point where you become so zapped of energy that you can't even get out of bed. Burnout does impact some people in that way and it's undeniable when you have reached that point. Taking a few days or weeks off at that stage won't be enough to replenish your fuel tanks. Your mental resilience will collapse into a heap at the first challenge upon your return. You're not only out of gas but you've seized your engine! It can take months to get your zest back if you have burned out to that extent.

Then there is another, more insidious form of burnout that is not as easily recognized. It's when you keep getting out of bed and going through the motions out of a sense of obligation. You become robotic in fulfilling your responsibilities. You continue to 'operate' but without passion and joy. You keep going because you are too tired to change. People can operate like this for years. The devastating aspect to this type of burnout is that if you stay in this state for long enough, it becomes the new you. The real you—the passionate, fun, spontaneous you—becomes lost to your memory. A robotic and passionless life becomes normal.

If any of this sounds too familiar, take heart because most high level achievers have burned out at least once in their journey. It's not the end of the road for you; it just marks the end of you being able to do life in that way. Often, it's only when you find yourself out of fuel and in a ditch, that you recognize what are your personal 'add fuel' warning signals. Once you've recovered, and you will recover, you'll be more conscious of your fuel levels and the associated warning signals.

A 6:1 Ratio

There is something to a six to one ratio. Work hard for six days and take one day to completely relax. Extrapolate that out. Work hard for six weeks and completely relax for one week. Work hard for six years and take one full year off. Wow! Doesn't that sound good? What fun things would you do with a whole year off? With all your responsibilities it may not be practical but you have to admit that it resonates with your imagination doesn't it? Most people's rhythm is to work like crazy and rest when they are too worn out to continue.

The six to one ratio may not be appropriate for you but it is an example of an exertion/relaxation rhythm. Find your rhythm and never have to worry about running out of gas on your road to success. I think Leonardo Da Vinci sums it up the best, "Every now and then go away, have a little relaxation, for when you come back to your work your judgment will be surer. Go some distance away because then the work appears smaller and more of it can be taken in at a glance and a lack of harmony and proportion is more readily seen."

—⚬⚬⚬—

Now to the How To: Rest

1. Redefine rest as an investment in productivity not recovery from tiredness.

2. Establish a routine for rest. Do not leave rest for when the work is done.

3. Discern what your 'add fuel' warnings are and heed them.

4. If you are burned out, don't try and soldier on. Get some counseling and establish a recovery plan. You're not a failure, it's just that your process is deficient.

5. Book your breaks first and then fit your work around them. Don't wait for a lull in your schedule before you go on a break. Look after you first because you're of little value to anyone when you're as dry as burned toast.

Quick Fuel: Rest

Fatigue makes cowards of us all. *George S. Patton, Jr.*

The time to relax is when you don't have time for it. *Sidney J. Harris*

Rest is not quitting the busy career; rest is the fitting of self to its sphere. *John Sullivan Dwight*

Sometimes the most urgent and vital thing you can possibly do is take a complete rest. *Ashleigh Brilliant*

Take care of your body. It's the only place you have to live. *Jim Rohn*

Rest is not idleness, and to lie sometimes on the grass under the trees on a summer's day, listening to the murmur of water, or watching the clouds float across the sky, is by no means a waste of time. *John Lubbock*

I still need more healthy rest in order to work at my best. My health is the main capital I have and I want to administer it intelligently. *Ernest Hemingway*

The idle man does not know what it is to enjoy rest. *Albert Einstein*

Put off thy cares with thy clothes; so shall thy rest strengthen thy labor, and so thy labor sweeten thy rest. *Richard Quarles*

Take rest; a field that has rested gives a bountiful crop. *Ovid*

Success Workshop: Rest

1. Do you find it easy to organize breaks or is getting away from the action always a challenge to you?

_____

2. What is the longest, most restful break that you have ever had?

_____

_____

3. If money was no issue and your responsibilities could be left in reliable hands, where would you go for a complete rest?

_____

_____

4. What stops you from doing the above?

_____

_____

_____

5. How many times a year would you like to enjoy a restful vacation and for how long each time? Is it possible that you could achieve it if you set your mind and business to achieving it?

_____

_____

_____

Conclusion

―――◦◦◦―――

You are not made powerless by your conditions; you are made powerful by the amount of fuel in your tanks. Your onboard energy is the key to overriding the prevailing conditions. The fuel inside of you is the key to dealing with the challenges outside of you. Don't wait until you feel like it before you refuel. Be proficient at knowing where your fuel comes from and fill up on it regularly.

1. Recommit everyday to the essentials:

> Attitude - Choose to be positive. Don't let your mind be governed by circumstances.

> Belief - Stop being double-minded. Believe in your self and act like you do.

> Confidence - Build your confidence. Protect it and don't neglect it.

> Drive - Serve a dream so compelling you are motivated to get up early and work late.

> Enthusiasm - Be enthusiastic by choice and not by needing the right conditions.

> Focus - Know what you want. Focus your power on it and stop getting distracted.

2. Reading: Transform your future by reading books that transform your mind.

3. Resources: Create spread, financial reserves, and non-personal exertion income.

4. Realizations: Take notice of your realizations and empower them to change you.

5. Relationships: Don't leave relationships to chance. Proactively build a people bank.

6. Results: Never let floundering become normal. Create a results momentum.

7. Rest: Know your exertion/relaxation rhythm. Use rest to increase the potency of your productivity.

Keep in mind that being full of fuel is not your ultimate goal. Nobody is going to pay you for full fuel tanks. They will pay you for providing a service, supplying a product, filling a need, increasing revenue, and causing growth. Fuel is what gets you through the obstacles that are between you and the achievement of these things. Fuel energizes you to stay motivated, resilient, and on course.

Respond to challenges by adding fuel. Gravity stops a lot of people but it need not stop you. Big dreams are out there. With enough fuel, you will burst right through gravity and reach those dreams.

Add Fuel

When you're traveling along in pursuit of your goal
The headwinds of life will take their toll
You will become weary and slow in your pace
Then start to question, 'Do I have what it takes?'
Your vision so clear gets lost in confusion
Doubts take control with their anxious conclusions
But it's not that you're weak and by no means a fool
It's simply a sign that it's time to add fuel

Your dream is a good one—it will buy you the bank
But you're not going to get there just on one tank
Pump yourself up every hour if you need
Fill up your mind and regain your speed
There will always be forces between you and the top
That can slow down your progress and tempt you to stop
But you will be the winner—for when you got low—
You filled up with fuel and got back on the go!

-Wes Beavis-

www.WesBeavis.com

1-877-Wes-Book